Operation *Barbarossa* 1941 (3)

Army Group Center

Campaign • 186

Operation *Barbarossa* 1941 (3)

Army Group Center

Robert Kirchubel • Illustrated by Peter Dennis

First published in Great Britain in 2007 by Osprey Publishing,
Midland House, West Way, Botley, Oxford OX2 0PH, UK
44-02 23rd St, Suite 219, Long Island City, NY 11101, USA

ISBN 978 1 84603 107 6

Page layout by The Black Spot
Index by Alison Worthington
Maps by The Map Studio Ltd
3D bird's-eye views by The Black Spot
Battlescene illustrations by Peter Dennis
Originated by United Graphics Pte Ltd, Singapore
Printed in China through World Print Ltd.
Typeset in Helvetica Neue and ITC New Baskerville

10 11 12 13 14   12 11 10 9 8 7 6 5 4 3

A CIP catalog record for this book is available from the British Library

FOR A CATALOG OF ALL BOOKS PUBLISHED BY OSPREY MILITARY
AND AVIATION PLEASE CONTACT:

Osprey Direct, c/o Random House Distribution Center,
400 Hahn Road, Westminster, MD 21157
E-mail: uscustomerservice@ospreypublishing.com

Osprey Direct, The Book Service Ltd, Distribution Centre,
Colchester Road, Frating Green, Colchester, Essex, CO7 7DW
E-mail: customerservice@ospreypublishing.com

www.ospreypublishing.com

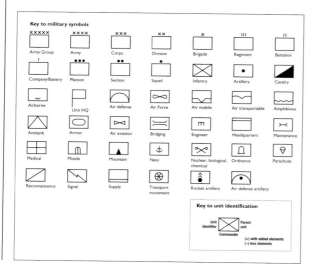

Key to military symbols

Author's note

This book is written to the glory of God. I wish to thank my wife
Linda and sons Mason and Marc for their support. Friends Joe
Wilson and Gary Komar helped greatly with editing and content.
The Interlibrary Loan Department at Fresno State University
provided valuable assistance. Ian Baxter at HITM was a gentleman
to work with, and Nino Savatte motivated me.

The title of this trilogy of Campaign titles is "Operation *Barbarossa*,"
not "The Soviet Defense of the Motherland." In considerable part
this is due to the fact that I speak and read German, therefore any
non-English sources were in German rather than Russian. However,
I believe that I have been true to the historian's responsibility to
maintain impartial objectivity, and have described events as the
facts warrant.

In about 1980, as a US Army armor officer in Germany, I sat on my
tank alongside a country road during a pause in the usual autumn
maneuvers (REFORGER). An old *Ostheer* veteran came over struck
up a conversation. Describing *Barbarossa*, he said "*Dass war eine'
Leistung!*" – "That was quite a performance!" While I still agree with
him, in the final analysis the Nazi–Soviet War was also clearly a
tremendous Soviet victory.

The following abbreviations are used for photographic sources:
HITM: History in the Making
Ralph Ingersoll Collection: From the Ralph Ingersoll Collection in the
    Howard Gottlieb Archival Research Center at Boston University
NARA: US National Archives and Records Administration
Podzun: Podzun Verlag, Friedburg, Germany
USAMHI: US Army Military History Institute

Artist's note

Readers may care to note that the original paintings from which the
colour plates in this book were prepared are available for private
sale. All reproduction copyright whatsoever is retained by the
Publishers. All inquiries should be addressed to:

Peter Dennis
Fieldhead,
The Park, Mansfield,
Nottinghamshire
NG18 2AT,
UK

The Publishers regret that they can enter into no correspondence
upon this matter.

CONTENTS

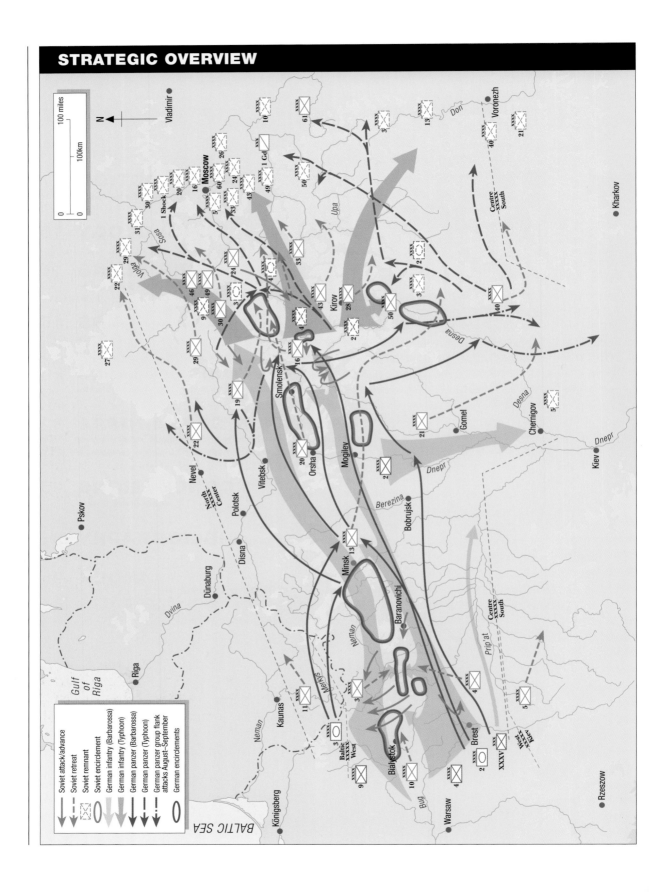

INTRODUCTION

The Nazis' decisions concerning Moscow are among the most hotly debated aspects of World War II. Stalin's capital never figured prominently in Hitler's concept of *Barbarossa*: it was not an initial objective, like destroying the bulk of the Red Army west of the Dvina and Dnepr. Neither was Moscow the ultimate geographic objective of the invasion, which was the Archangel–Astrakhan line. After all, the Wehrmacht had essentially defeated both Poland and France before either Warsaw or Paris had fallen; the capture of capital cities merely represented political formalities. Clearly, many German generals thought differently, the principal among them being Army Chief of Staff General Franz Halder. Below the Führer and Halder stood operational leaders of armies and corps who, with their soldiers on the ground, simply wanted firm and unconflicting guidance from above.

It was Field Marshal Fedor von Bock who would lead Army Group Center, the *Schwerpunkt* or decisive element of the *Barbarossa* plan, toward Moscow. The Germans attacked generally along the relatively high ground that divided the watersheds of the Dvina and Dnepr rivers – the same route followed by Napoleon in his fateful 1812 invasion. Von Bock had proved himself in Germany's earlier Blitzkrieg campaigns, and was well resourced; his command comprised Fourth and Ninth Armies and two armored groups, plus the Luftwaffe's premier close air support formation.

Within hours of the German invasion opening, American political cartoonist Theodor Geissel ("Dr Seuss") recognized that the war in the East would be a far different matter from Hitler's earlier invasions. Note that Italy is portrayed in the middle of the Führer's wall of trophies as a road-kill skunk. (Ralph Ingersoll Collection)

Field Marshal Fedor von Bock expected to be able to run Army Group Center in accordance with Prussian traditions of operational freedom. In practice he had to overcome interference from Hitler and, just as often, from Army Chief of Staff Halder. (NARA)

After Stalin's central European land grab in 1939–40, the Red Army in Poland stood closer to Berlin than to Moscow. However, the bulk of the Western Special Military District (WSMD – "Special" meaning that it could supposedly fight without substantial reinforcement) occupied dangerously exposed positions in the Bialystok salient between East Prussia and occupied southern Poland. Since the acquisition of these territories had represented the high point of Soviet interwar foreign policy, Stalin insisted that Colonel-General D.G. Pavlov, commanding WSMD, fight hard to keep them. One of the few Soviet veterans of the Spanish Civil War to survive Stalin's purges, Pavlov's was a secondary command, since the dictator expected the Germans' main blow to fall in the Ukraine. Von Bock outclassed Pavlov in every way, and, although Bolshevik theorists had predicted the "Second Imperialist War" since the days of Lenin, the unleashing of *Barbarossa* achieved total surprise against Pavlov, as against his fellow commanders elsewhere.

ORIGINS OF THE CAMPAIGN[1]

On the day before the invasion, People's Commissar for Internal Affairs L.P. Beria wrote to Stalin, agreeing with his master that "Hitler is not going to attack us in 1941." Although Stalin was surprised by the timing, the axis of the main attacks and the ferocity of *Barbarossa*, in fact he had probably expected an eventual German invasion. By signing the Molotov–Ribbentrop Treaty in August 1939, which provided Germany with natural resources, strategic materials and a free hand in western and much of central Europe, Stalin had bought time – but his misjudgement over how much time was nearly to prove fatal. By mid-winter 1940 the continued German air blitz on Britain represented merely a convenient cover story for preparations for *Barbarossa*. The final straw came in November: first, Franklin D. Roosevelt won re-election as US President, thus ruling out American isolationism for much longer; and then Soviet Foreign Minister V.M. Molotov paid a return visit to Berlin. Hitler needed to decide once and for all if Stalin's wider aims clashed or coincided with his own. Molotov, initially wanting to continue appeasing Germany, attempted to talk specifics, but Hitler tried vaguely to point the USSR toward feasting on British interests in southwest Asia. In fact he considered the talks a charade, simultaneously telling his staff that "preparations for the East are to be continued." For his part, Stalin no longer harbored any illusions about the ultimate future relationship with Nazi Germany, although he disastrously underestimated the imminence of the threat.

After nearly two decades of Nazi ranting about a Jewish–Bolshevik conspiracy and demands for *Lebensraum*, with a German economic catastrophe impending, and the impossibility of an invasion of Britain undeniable, Hitler signed the *Barbarossa* directive five weeks after Molotov departed Berlin. In the spring of 1941 he put his personal imprint on the character of the impending eastern campaign with three policy documents.

The first was the March 13, 1941 publication of an annex to the operations order by which Hitler rejected army administration of occupied areas, turning these duties over to Nazi Party and police organs. Reichsführer-SS Heinrich Himmler received "special tasks," including the creation of *Einsatzgruppen* that would follow the army to round up and murder Jews, Communists and other enemies of the *Volk*. Hitler augmented this annex on May 13 with his "Decree on Military Justice" (sic), relieving military commanders of responsibility for prosecuting their own war criminals; and again on June 6, with the better-known "Commissar Order." These documents can be considered as the beginning of a second Nazi revolution: henceforth Germany's conduct of the war took on a new and darker complexion. Taken together with her general occupation practices and her brutal treatment of Soviet POWs, they mark spring 1941 as the date when Germany began to sink toward Auschwitz.

The stage was set for history's greatest campaign. Fringe historians perpetuate unsubstantiated rumors that Stalin was preparing for his own pre-emptive attack. The Soviet General Staff naturally had contingency plans for an attack against Germany, but there is no evidence that these had any effect on German planning. As with Hitler's every aggressive act since the fairy-tale wars of the Rhineland, Austria and Czechoslovakia, *Barbarossa* was purely a war of conquest.

Meanwhile, Stalin appeared to be blissfully ignorant of the impending war. The undisputed fount of all Soviet domestic and foreign policy and military decision-making, he was not the first European leader to misjudge Hitler, and within the Soviet hierarchy he had many equally unprepared accomplices in state, party, diplomatic and military circles. His much criticized signing of the Nonaggression Pact with Hitler in 1939 and the Economic Accord the following January kept the USSR out of the pan-European war for nearly two years, and the Neutrality Pact negotiated with Japan on April 13, 1940 was equally significant. While the Soviets had to keep a wary eye on Japan's 39 divisions, 1,200 tanks and 2,500 aircraft in Manchuria during the first half of *Barbarossa*, Stalin's staff could be reasonably sure that they only had to plan for a one-front war. Like the Germans, the Soviet leaders had a long time to prepare for *Barbarossa*.

Lieutenant- General I.V. Boldin, Commander of the 50th Army. Boldin escaped from the Minsk pocket in July 1941 and the Vyazma pocket in October 1941. His dogged defense of Tula and persistent counterattacks against Guderian's left flank doomed the German southern pincer against Moscow. (David Glantz)

---

1 For reasons of space, we do not repeat here the various points about the deeper background to the Nazi–Soviet War, and Hitler's pre-*Barbarossa* geo-political calculations, that may be found in the introductory material to the first two titles in this trilogy: Campaigns 129 *Operation Barbarossa (1) Army Group South*, and 148 *(2) Army Group North*.

CHRONOLOGY

(Most events leading up to Barbarossa *are covered in the Chronology sections of the titles Campaign 129 & 148)*

1941

February 20 Göring creates Luftwaffe planning staff for *Barbarossa*.
June 22–30 Battle for Fortress Brest.
June 23–25 Boldin's counterattack at Grodno.
June 24 LVII Panzer Corps captures Vilnius.
June 28–29 20th & 18th Panzer Divisions close Minsk *Kessel*.
June 30 Hoth and Guderian confer. OKH directs Von Bock to advance on Smolensk.
July 3–27 Von Kluge commands Fourth Panzer Army.
July 4 3rd Panzer Division captures Dnepr bridge at Rogatchev.
July 8 20th Panzer Division captures Dvina bridge at Ulla.
July 12 Stavka orders Timoshenko to organize counterattacks toward Bobruisk and prepare defense of Mogilev.
July 15 7th Panzer Division captures Yartsevo, isolating Smolensk.
July 16 29th Motorized Division enters Smolensk, completing "loose" encirclement.
July 17–27 Battle for Mogilev after Soviets frustrate initial German attempts to lever River Dnepr.
July 20 10th Panzer Division occupies Yelnia.
July 21–July 22 Luftwaffe initiates bombing of Moscow.
July 23–August 7 Timoshenko counteroffensive – Group Kachalov
July 24–27 Timoshenko counteroffensive – Groups Kalinin & Khomenko, plus Gorodovikov's cavalry raid.
July 29–31 Timoshenko counteroffensive – Group Maslinnikov.
August 3 IX Army & XXIV Panzer Corps encircle Roslavl.
August 5 Germans consider battle for Smolensk to be over.
August 11 Soviets begin general offensive around Yelnia.
August 19 XXIV Panzer Corps plus VII & XIII Army Corps capture Gomel.
September 6 Soviets re-occupy Yelnia. Hitler issues his Directive 35.
September 7 XIII, XLIII & XXXV Army Corps capture Chernigov.
September 10 Stavka instructs forces before Moscow to transition to defense.
September 30 & October 2 Army Group Center begins Operation *Typhoon*.
October 7 7th & 10th Panzer Divisions close Viazma *Kessel*. Beginning of *rasputitsa,* and first snowfalls.
October 8 XLVII Panzer Corps & LIII Army Corps close Bryansk *Kessel*.
October 8, 9 & 19 Soviets issue various directives on defense of Moscow.
October 11–16 First battle of Mozhaisk line ends in stalemate. Town of Mozhaisk falls on 19th.
October 13 Kaluga falls.
October 14 1st Panzer Division enters Kalinin.
November 13 Halder hosts conference of *Ostheer* chiefs of staff at Orsha.
November 14 & 16 November Zhukov launches pre-emptive attacks against Army Group Center.
November 15 Von Bock's left wing begins Operation *Volga Reservoir*.
November 18 Guderian launches final assault south of Moscow.
November 22 Klin falls.
November 25 17th Panzer Division reaches Kashira – Guderian's farthest advance.

OPPOSING PLANS

GERMAN PLANS

Flushed with victory after crushing France, Hitler had wanted to invade the USSR in autumn 1940 – an ambition vigorously opposed by his generals. This disagreement, and logistical weakness and delays, convinced Hitler to postpone the assault until the following spring. The dominating role of logistics was underlined on July 21, 1940 when the army commander-in-chief, Field Marshal Walther von Brauchitsch, told Hitler that only 80–100 divisions would be required to subdue the Soviets – a number in fact largely dictated by what the Deutsche Reichsbahn could move and sustain, rather than a realistic estimate.

In the opinion of Hitler and the Wehrmacht, a war against the USSR would be quick and easy; the Nazi ideology exaggerated Germany's prowess while minimizing that of her enemies. The Germans had nearly 11 months to plan *Barbarossa*, much longer than for their earlier campaigns, but in the event the staff work was far from flawless, and the resources were insufficient. The marching army did not have the capacity simultaneously to penetrate the Soviet lines and to conduct huge encirclements much beyond the frontier – indeed, it is questionable if even a fully-motorized force, like the US Army in 1944–45, could have done what the Wehrmacht expected of the Ostheer in *Barbarossa*.

Many details of German planning for *Barbarossa* have been discussed in the earlier titles of this trilogy, and reviewing a few points will suffice. For example, the initially competing plans of OKH (Army High Command) and OKW (Armed Forces High Command) only came together in the autumn of 1940, and operational staffs created detailed directives and operations orders during the following winter and spring. However, the Germans' traditional emphasis on operations hamstrung

Bicycle infantry still made up a significant part of the strength of German infantry division reconnaissance units. These soldiers, with their comrades on horses, motorcycles and in light armoured and field cars, were often far ahead of the foot-sloggers, and carried much of the burden of fighting on first contact. (HITM)

A scene repeated countless times during Operation *Barbarossa*: a *frontovik* who has given his all defending the motherland. The ordinary German and Russian junior rank – the *Landser* and *frontovik* – fought and tried to survive in very similar conditions. Both served regimes led by dictators of boundless wickedness and violence. Both fought boldly in the attack and tenaciously in defense. Summer heat and winter cold affected them equally; the dust or mud were just as bad on each side of the lines, and poor food, inadequate medical care, lack of home leave and abundance of vermin made life miserable for the fighting men of both armies. (Elukka)

the planning for personnel, military intelligence and logistics, especially given the unrealistic assumptions about *Barbarossa*'s expected length – of between six and ten weeks only. Also, the massive size of the Eastern Front would dramatically decrease German weapon densities: they could count on one tank per 29 square miles in the West, but in the East this fell to one per 112 square miles. Above the battlefield, the ratio plummeted from one aircraft per 20 square miles in 1940, to one per 95 square miles during *Barbarossa*.

Military intelligence, historically a weakness of German operational staffs, was abysmal for *Barbarossa*. Lieutenant-Colonel Eberhard Kinzel's analysis of the Red Army was deeply flawed; for example, his staff overestimated Pavlov's infantry by 40 percent while underestimating his armored and mechanized forces by 70–80 percent.

Although Hermann Göring correctly predicted in February 1941 that logistics would "endanger the entire operation," this aspect of planning was equally inadequate. The staff assumed that the roads and railroads west of the Dvina and Dnepr rivers would be superior to those east of that line; but this was true only in a very relative sense, and movement capability became a limiting factor as soon as the Germans crossed the frontier. Logistics were also one main reason for locating *Barbarossa*'s *Schwerpunkt* in the center: German rail connections from the Reich to East Prussia and occupied Poland – which also offered better staging areas for a potential attack on the Moscow axis – were superior to those farther south in Hungary and Romania.

Halder gave General Paulus the task of developing the Marcks Plan when the latter became *Oberquartiermeister I* on September 3. Paulus finished this work in just two weeks, presenting his own "Foundations of the Russian Operation" at the end of October. Wargames tested these plans from November 29 to December 3. Von Brauchitsch told his staff to expect "a hefty border fight" lasting some four weeks, after which the remainder of the USSR would be occupied against only "weak resistance." The overview portion of the OKH *Aufmarschanweisung* mentioned Moscow as an objective of Von Bock's command only after resistance in the North had been broken, and specific instructions for his army group did not mention the Soviet capital.[2]

Army Group Center, under Von Bock from September 20 1940, received the mission of destroying Red Army forces in Belorussia. Panzer groups on the flanks represented Von Bock's main punch, with infantry armies marching in between. After encircling an initial *Kessel* ("cauldron," i.e. pocket) at Minsk, Army Group Center's operational goals were Vitebsk and Orsha (the Dvina–Dnepr line), to be followed by a three-week logistical pause for the "railroad advance." The outer wings would then swing wide and meet again to create another pocket at Smolensk. Victory was universally defined as destruction of the Red Army west of the Dvina and Dnepr. A major adjustment occurred on March 8, 1941 when Hitler directed (1) that an infantry corps be detailed for security duty on the army group's right, bordering the Rokitno Marshes, and (2) that the strategic reserves would follow Von Bock. These formations, generally under Second Army, quickly became a de facto part of Army Group Center, and the General Headquarters ceased to have any reserves worthy of the name.

While acknowledging the benefits to the defense of numerous rivers, Colonel-General Hermann Hoth's own *Aufmarschanweisung* urged his Third Panzer Group go "eastwards fast and without looking back," to wreak havoc on enemy command and control, reinforcements and logistics. Third Panzer Group would initially be under Ninth Army control. Colonel-General Guderian hoped to reach Minsk with his Second Panzer Group in five or six days; this formation fell under Fourth Army, which also had the missions of defending against a surprise Soviet invasion to the west, and helping close off any encirclements. After taking Smolensk, both strategic and operational leaders anticipated that Army Group Center would turn north toward Leningrad.

The German Air Force completed its plans for *Barbarossa* on February 20. The Luftwaffe possessed the same concepts of *Vernichtungskrieg*, *Auftragstaktik* and *Schwerpunkt* as the army. It also shared the army's weakness of having very junior officers plan such a massive undertaking as *Barbarossa* (who provided sealed orders to Luftwaffe crews that were to be opened only eight hours prior to H-Hour!). Air superiority was its first priority. The Luftwaffe sought first to destroy the Red Army Air Force

No way for a modern army to conquer the planet's largest nation: a German column with commandeered local pony-sledges plods eastward during the coldest winter in many years. Despite ample experience in the East during the Great War, Germany's curious neglect of logistic in favor of operational planning was a weakness that would be exposed on the first day of the campaign, and would haunt its every step thereafter. (HITM)

During a pause in their advance eastward, men of a Panzer unit watch a flight of Ju 87B Stukas land at an improvised airfield. While such an open landscape might be familiar to a Russian or North American, it was psychologically overwhelming to the Germans. (HITM)

German army logistics elements lagged far behind combat units, and were often relegated to the worst "roads" – with dire consequences, given the Wehrmacht's heavy reliance on horse transport. It was not only the mud of the autumn and spring rainy seasons that imprisoned wagon wheels and wore down horses; the choking dust and deep, concrete-hard ruts of summer were also destructive. (HITM)

(especially its most modern equipment) and its supporting ground operations. Assisted by Lufthansa pilots gathering data during civilian flights over the USSR, the Germans had very good intelligence on Soviet dispositions. However, owing to range and payload limitations, the Luftwaffe could not attack the Soviet aviation industry effectively. After gaining air superiority the Luftwaffe would shift to flying close air support missions for the army – its main mission.

SOVIET PLANS

The Soviet High Command had watched Hitler dismember Poland, France and numerous smaller opponents, yet they had no workable plan to counter the Blitzkrieg. Sensing that an upcoming conflict would be a war of attrition, with resource-poor Germany aiming for the Ukraine, on October 5, 1940 Stalin ordered the main Soviet defensive effort redirected south away from the Moscow axis. This ignored the fact that communications in southern Poland and Romania were too bad, and the Balkans too insecure, for that area ever to support the *Schwerpunkt* of *Barbarossa*. Pavlov, the WSMD commander, thus lost the status and resources of the main defensive effort.

A good idea of the complexity of bridge-building in order to cross Russia's many and often wide rivers can be gained from this collection of combat vehicles, trucks and trailers, timber and watercraft photographed by the River Bug in June 1941. (HITM)

Soviet planning went ahead when Stalin summoned the Politburo and military leaders to a ten-day conference in Moscow starting on December 23, 1940. Wargames followed immediately, with General G.K. Zhukov teamed with 21 other generals to simulate an attack on WSMD, against Pavlov plus 28 other generals. From January 2 to 6, Zhukov led the "Germans" out of Prussia and Poland, and these maneuvers exposed the vulnerability of Pavlov's four armies to encirclement. When roles were reversed, Zhukov easily parried Pavlov's mechanized attack into Germany – causing the Soviet leadership to question the wisdom of its strategic "Red Folder" counteroffensive plans, but not with sufficient vigor.

The Soviets' sanguine assumptions about the outcome of their wargames matched those of the Germans about theirs. Red Army defenses were revealed to be only one echelon deep and lacking reserves, but these facts did not trouble the national leadership. Significant forces still occupied the massive Bialystok salient, ripe for Von Bock's picking; WSMD occupied a 270-mile front, most of it along this treacherous bulge. According to John Erickson, Pavlov's main contribution to his defensive capability during the months before *Barbarossa* was to tweak a few unit dispositions, in the process weakening the line and depriving his forces of reserves of their own. This was most noticeable on the very axis that Guderian would use, but it was approved by the Soviet high command.

The WSMD issued its Order 008130 on March 26, 1941, ordering all units to achieve full strength by June 15, but resources fell far short of good intentions. It is very likely that in the minds of Stalin and Zhukov WSMD existed as a sacrifice to the Blitzkrieg; by February 1941 they may already have been thinking that the Reserve Front might fight the main defensive battle along the pre-1939 frontier and the "Stalin Line." Pavlov's bad luck would continue.

---

2 In the German staff system a directive (*Weisung*) did not have the force of an order (*Befehl*).

OPPOSING COMMANDERS

GERMAN COMMANDERS

The 64-year-old **Field Marshal Fedor von Bock**, commanding Army Group Center, has been described as a "difficult man." In April 1918 Major von Bock had earned the *Pour le Mérite* for "reckless bravery." He spoke French fluently and English and Russian well. He seems to have been neutral about the Nazi seizure of power. Von Bock led Army Group North in 1939 and Army Group B in Holland and Belgium. Usually "the stoic guardsman," he was the only senior leader to question *Barbarossa* when briefed on its plan in January 1941. Hitler relieved him of command of Army Group Center on December 19, 1941, but a month later recalled him to lead Army Group South. Unsatisfactory progress in Operation *Blau* caused Hitler to relieve Von Bock for good in July 1942. He was killed with his wife and stepdaughter when Royal Air Force aircraft strafed road traffic on May 2, 1945.

Third Panzer Group commander **Colonel-General Hermann Hoth** is one of the Wehrmacht's most underrated generals. He commanded XV Motorized (Panzer) Corps with distinction during the Polish and western campaigns. In October 1941 he took over Seventeenth Army in the Ukraine. Starting in July 1942, he commanded Fourth Panzer Army, which he led toward Stalingrad in the attempted relief of Sixth Army, in Operation *Backhand Blow*, and in the *Schwerpunkt* of Operation *Citadel*'s southern wing in July 1943. Hitler relieved Hoth in December 1943, making him a scapegoat for the loss of Kiev, and never recalled him.

Colonel-General Adolf Strauss had commanded Ninth Army under Von Bock since the western campaign. He trained his army to be the first wave of the stillborn Operation *Sealion* against Britain, until transferred east for *Barbarossa*. He led the Ninth with ability until January 12, 1942, when he asked to be relieved "for health reasons." Thereafter he sat out the rest of the war.

One of two field marshals to command a field army during *Barbarossa*, **Günther Hans von Kluge** led Fourth Army as he had in Poland and France. An artillery officer since the Great War, he resigned in 1938–39 over Hitler's aggressive policies. He took command of Army Group Center upon Von Bock's removal, and undoubtedly came under the spell of the anti-Hitler conspirators rampant there. He led that organization in Operation *Citadel*, but was severely injured in an automobile crash in October 1943. He came out of hospital the following July just in time to replace Gerd von Rundstedt as Supreme Commander/West. He lasted in that post only until the next month when, suspected by Hitler of negotiating with the western allies, he took poison.

Colonel-General Heinz Guderian, commander in 1941 of Second Panzer Group, is one of the war's best-known generals. During the Great

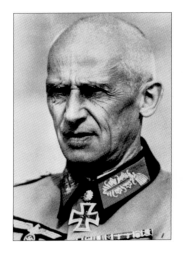

Colonel-General Hermann "Papa" Hoth proved himself to be an exceptionally reliable commander from the outbreak of the war until 1943. A team player and a good man in a crisis, the commander of the Third Panzer Group suffered from few of Guderian's prima donna tendencies, and adhered better to *Barbarossa*'s plans and Von Bock's orders. (USAMHI)

War and the Weimar period his experience of Jäger, signal and transport duties, service with the Freikorps and training at Kazan, USSR, prepared him to become one of the world's foremost theorists and practitioners of armored warfare. Perhaps because of this, he could act like a prima donna who refused to subordinate his desire for personal glory to the higher strategic purpose. He commanded XIX Motorized (Panzer) Corps in Poland and France. At Von Kluge's urging, Hitler relieved him of command of Second Panzer Group on Christmas Day 1941. Guderian became Inspector General of Panzer Troops in February 1943. The Führer made him Chief of the German General Staff the day following the July 1944 assassination attempt, a position he held until March 1945.

Colonel-General Maximilian *Reichsfreiherr* von Weichs commanded Second Army. A Bavarian cavalry captain in World War I, he was the first commander of 1st Panzer Division. Von Weichs commanded XIII Corps during the Anschluss, against Czechoslovakia and in Poland, then led the Second Army in France and the Balkan campaigns. He later led the northern wing of Operation *Blau* against Stalingrad, earning promotion to field marshal in February 1943 despite his questionable leadership during the Stalingrad crisis. Thereafter he commanded the German defense of Greece and Yugoslavia through 1944, until sent to Führer Reserve in March 1945.

Second Air Fleet commander **Field Marshal Albert Kesselring** started as a Bavarian artillery officer during the Great War, rising to the rank of army colonel in 1931; transferred to the Luftwaffe in 1933, within two years he became its chief of staff. He led Germany's largest aerial formations from Poland throughout *Barbarossa*. In November 1941 he (and many of his units) transferred to Italy, where he became the Axis Supreme Commander/South. He held this position, very ably, through the North African, Sicilian and most of the Italian campaigns. His final assignment as Supreme Commander/West came in January 1945 after Hitler relieved Von Rundstedt for the last time.

The cruel realities of *Barbarossa* completely outclassed Colonel-General of Tank Troops D.G. Pavlov who was equivalent to a man who brought a knife to a gun fight. Within a month Stalin had Pavlov, Pavlov's chief of staff and 4th Army commander Korobkov standing before firing squads. (Corbis)

The pitiless realities of the attempts to halt Von Bock's assaults almost cost 19th Army commander Lieutenant-General I.S. Konev his job (and perhaps his life?) within weeks of his arrival on the Moscow axis. He soon regained his balance, and went on to become one of Stalin's best operational commanders. (Elukka)

Colonel-General Wolfram *Freiherr* von Richthofen commanded the elite VIII Fliegerkorps. A World War I cavalry officer, he was a civilian engineer during the Weimar years and transferred to the new Luftwaffe in 1933, within two years serving as the Condor Legion's chief of staff. Judging that strategic bombing would not win the war for Franco, he perfected close air support instead, developing and improving its planning, communications and liaison with ground troops. He led his air corps from Poland and, in *Barbarossa*, served in the Mediterranean theater, in the Crimea and during the Stalingrad relief effort, and became a field marshal in February 1943. He was diagnosed with a brain tumor in October 1944, and died in captivity nine months later.

The smaller II Fliegerkorps was commanded by **Colonel-General Bruno Loerzer**, a 44-victory World War I ace and *Pour le Mérite* recipient. A lifelong personal friend of Hermann Göring, he was a leader of average talents, who did show some intelligent interest in ground support operations. His air corps was transferred to the Mediterranean in October 1941.

SOVIET COMMANDERS

Colonel-General of Tank Troops D.G. Pavlov, the luckless commander of WSMD and the 671,165-man West Front, was cruelly nicknamed "the Soviet Guderian." He had served in the Spanish Civil War, but mislearned its lessons: he judged that armored forces were not suited to large formations, and that the Red Army's tanks should supplement rifle divisions in battalion strength. He did lead Soviet armor against Vyborg in the closing days of the Winter War in Finland. During the last hours of peace he was enjoying comedy theater at the Minsk Officers Club, and dismissed (literally) eleventh-hour warnings that night as rumors. He was arrested for "disgraceful cowardice, negligence, breakdown in command and control;" Stalin had Pavlov shot in late July, but Khrushchev posthumously rehabilitated his reputation in 1956.

The 3rd Army commander **Lieutenant-General V.I. Kuznetsov** managed to survive *Barbarossa*. He went on to lead the 21st, 58th, 1st Shock, 4th Reserve, 63rd (at Stalingrad), 1st Guards and 3rd Shock armies. In this final assignment his soldiers captured the Reichstag in May 1945.

The 4th Army commander **Major-General A.A. Korobkov** suffered the same fate as his superior Pavlov; Korobkov never had control over his organization, but was executed as a traitor nonetheless.

Major-General K.D. Golubev initially commanded 10th Army. Later in *Barbarossa* he took over 43rd Army, remaining in command until severely wounded in action in 1944.

The following corps commanders did not survive Operation *Barbarossa*: **Major-Generals V.B. Borisov** (21st Rifle); **M.P. Petrov** (17th Mechanized, died of wounds); **F.D. Rubtsev** (1st Rifle, died in German captivity); **A.V. Garnov** (5th Rifle); **I.S. Nikitin** (6th Cavalry, executed in German captivity for "organizing an underground organization"); **M.G. Khatskilevich** (6th Mechanized, dead before the end of June).

In the wake of the unmitigated disasters which immediately befell the leaders of the West Front, a second echelon of commanders rose up. These included Red Army luminaries **Budenny**, **Timoshenko** and **Zhukov**. Unknown in 1941, but also significant later were the following:

The commander of a T-26 light tank surrenders to the command *"Hände hoch!"*. (Podzun)

Marshal S.M. Budenny had few qualifications for high-level command except for personal friendship with Stalin. His mediocre performance commanding the Reserve Front and subsequent disaster at Kiev quickly relegated him to secondary and ceremonial posts, as a new generation of combat-tested generals took over to defeat the Wehrmacht. His long survival was probably due to his stupidity – he could never be considered as a rival even during Stalin's worst fits of paranoia. (David Glantz)

Lieutenant-General I.V. Boldin, Pavlov's deputy was enjoying the same comedy play as his commander on June 21, but he managed to escape serving in close proximity to his superior. Boldin had served on the Turkish Front during World War I; he commanded mechanized forces that occupied eastern Poland in 1939, and the 9th Army which invaded Bessarabia a year later. During Operation *Typhoon* he commanded 50th Army, frustrating Guderian's attempts to take Tula. His soldiers recaptured Bryansk in 1943. Boldin is considered a mediocre general who used political acumen to keep his job until 1945.

Ukrainian **Lieutenant-General A.I. Yeremenko** arrived at the West Front on June 29 and immediately went to work. Wounded in action in October, he spent nearly a year in hospital, and was then almost captured by German tanks near Stalingrad. After *Barbarossa* he went on to command the Southeast, Stalingrad, Southern, Kalinin, 2nd Baltic and 4th Ukrainian Fronts. Yeremenko earned promotion to marshal in 1958.

Major-General I.S. Konev spent *Barbarossa*'s first weeks away from the fighting, until called to command 19th Army. After his initial poor performances only Zhukov's personal intervention saved Konev from Stalin's wrath. By Operation *Citadel* he had regained the dictator's confidence, and he too commanded a large number of fronts after *Barbarossa*: West, Steppe, Northwest, 2nd and 1st Ukrainian. He and Zhukov raced for Berlin in 1945. A marshal in 1956, Konev commanded Soviet forces that crushed the Hungarian Uprising of that year.

Major-General K.K. Rokossovsky was also active in the central sector during *Barbarossa*, and is introduced in Campaign 129 in this series. Interestingly, he was Zhukov's superior during the 1930s while commanding 7th Samara Cavalry Division.

19

OPPOSING ARMIES

Again, the reader is directed to the equivalent chapters in both the earlier titles in this trilogy for much general material. Obviously, the German and Soviet Armies had many differences, most notably at the higher echelons; but one feature shared by both (and most others) is often overlooked: the large number of non-divisional units that made up the corps and higher formations. These combat support or combat service support units often doubled the number of men in a corps beyond those simply assigned to divisions. Together the synergistic effect of all the forces in a corps greatly multiplied its combat power beyond that of the divisions alone; by task-organizing these assets, the commander built his *Schwerpunkt*. The following chart shows units assigned to various headquarters (assume a similar organization in northern and southern theaters):

GERMAN	Arty Bn	Eng Bn	Flak Bn	AT Bn	Asslt gun Bn	Nebelwerfer Bn
Army Gp Ctr	–	2	0.33	–	–	1
Ninth Army	–	4	3.66	1	–	–
VIII Corps	14	8	1.66	–	1	2
XX Corps	7	3	–	–	1	–
Third Pz Gp	–	–	0.33	–	–	–
V Corps	2	3	–	–	–	–
VI Corps	2	7	0.66	–	–	–
XXXIX Pz Cps	3	2	3.66	1.33	–	1
LVII Pz Cps	3	1	3	–	–	–
Fourth Army	2	4	3.66	–	1	–
VII Corps	6	5	0.33	1	1	–
IX Corps	4	4	0.33	–	1	–
XIII Corps	–	2	–	–	–	–
XLIII Corps	4	4	1.33	–	–	–
Second Pz Gp	2	5.33	–	–	–	–
XII Corps	6.33	5	1.33	1	1	3
XXIV Pz Cps	3	4	–	1	–	0.33
XLVI Pz Cps	–	1	–	–	–	–
XLVII Pz Cps	4	1	–	1	–	0.66

SOVIET	Arty Rgt	Eng Rgt	AAA Rgt	AT Bde	Fortified Region
Front	12.66	5.33	0.33	1	5
3rd Army	2	–	0.33	1	1
4th Army	4	–	1	–	4
10th Army	7	–	0.66	1	1

GERMAN FORCES

National leadership

Mercifully for mankind, throughout two World Wars Germany's national leadership showed very little strategic skill. Neither the Kaiser and his generals nor the Führer and his showed much understanding of the wider world beyond Germany's immediate frontiers. The Oberkommando der

Wehrmacht (OKW) never managed to co-ordinate national political and economic objectives, nor Germany's four armed services (Army, Kriegsmarine, Luftwaffe, and Waffen-SS); it was intentionally kept weak in accordance with Hitler's leadership style.

Personalities at the top played critical roles. Hitler flaunted his lack of formal military training and operated primarily on intuition. In view of the racial, cultural and national importance he placed upon *Barbarossa* he set his imprint on that campaign more than any other, completely eclipsing every other member of the leadership. As a strategist, Luftwaffe commander Hermann Göring was an unqualified buffoon; Kriegsmarine commander Erich Raeder never played more than a marginal role, and Heinrich Himmler of the SS was militarily irrelevant in 1941.

Senior German army leaders were uniformly ineffectual. As professional head of the army, Von Brauchitsch peaked on November 5, 1939 when he stood up to Hitler. Completely unable to duplicate that feat, he slipped farther into the shadows over the next two years, finally retiring at the end of *Barbarossa* for health reasons. His chief of staff, Halder, worked tirelessly to advance his own agenda until replaced in September 1942. Supposedly Hitler's primary military adviser as chief of OKW, Field Marshal Wilhelm Keitel was a mere toady of the Führer, who failed his subordinates and his nation at every turn. The OKW operations chief, Colonel-General Alfred Jodl, practically worshipped Hitler, to the point where he lost all objectivity.

Doctrine

German success prior to *Barbarossa* rested on the weakness and disorganization of its enemies, and the Blitzkrieg. The vast extent of the USSR and the internal cohesion of the Communist state negated the former advantage, but the latter would still dominate land combat. The Blitzkrieg was never a doctrine in the sense of a system of theories and practices spelled out in German military manuals. The phrase seems to originate in attempts by contemporary western theorists to define Wehrmacht techniques in Poland and, later, the West. At the highest levels it was executed in discrete steps, isolating its victims and destroying them one by one; it is therefore more proper to speak of a Blitzkrieg campaign than of a Blitzkrieg war. This technique gave resource-poor Germany a way to fight a war on the cheap.

The Germans concentrated on *Waffenkrieg* (the operational level of war) and tactics. What written doctrine they did have, *Truppenführung* (Part I was unclassified and published in 1933), discussed leadership

Approximately 30 miles west of Moscow, reasonably well-clothed German infantry present a contrast with the usual image. A number of photographs of men from SS "Reich", in the Istra river sector during the mid-November actions against Rokossovsky's 16th Army, show them wearing white hooded smocks and trousers as well as the more common, long, snow-camouflage coats. Such clothing would not become general issue until the second winter of the Nazi–Soviet War. Right up to the gates of Moscow, Paul Hausser's men could be found in the thick of the fighting at Von Bock's center. (Podzun)

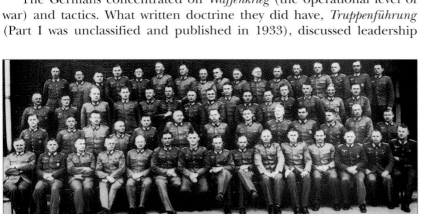

Sixty of the 73 officers of Infantry Regiment 12 (31st Infantry Division), photographed in April 1941 at Kutno in occupied Poland. By December the regiment would be on its fourth commander since the start of the campaign; its losses would also include the two majors shown here, two of the three captains, one of the five physicians, and 27 of the 56 lieutenants. (Podzun)

While *Landsers* in the foreground trudge past below a Panzer III, signal troops set up a radio with telescoping antenna. (HITM)

techniques the world would come to recognize as Blitzkrieg, but made very little mention of armored warfare or close air support. Once on the field of battle German officers applied this theory in combination with the independent *Stosstrupp* infiltration tactics of World War I, with General Hans von Seeckt's theories of combined arms, the meeting engagement and the *Schwerpunkt*, all wedded to the internal combustion engine and the radio in order to create the Blitzkrieg.

Panzers

German mechanization, especially in the form of tanks, was cutting-edge in the 1930s. The German Army experimented with armored warfare at their Grafenwöhr training area and during autumn maneuvers prior to 1932. Panzers gained essential political support during Guderian's famous demonstration in 1933, the year that Hitler came to power. Two years later the first three Panzer Divisions were established, and two years later still one made its debut at the autumn maneuvers. Despite impressive performances in 1939–40, one-quarter (683) of all the German tanks employed in the West in 1940 had been lost. In 1941, when the Wehrmacht still relied upon modestly updated versions of prewar designs that were at least equal to the great bulk of even older Soviet types, the Red Army was on the point of receiving a new and superior generation of tanks in the form of the T-34 medium and KV heavy designs. These would make their mark before the end of *Barbarossa*, and German inferiority in production capacity would soon prove equally significant.

Infantry

Despite the dominant position occupied by armoured divisions during World War II, it was this branch that bore the brunt of the Nazi–Soviet War. The *Ostheer* suffered 300,000 killed during *Barbarossa* – the equivalent of one regiment per day – and most of them were infantrymen. Except for the few who rode to battle with armored or motorized divisions the vast majority marched. Most carried a Mauser Kar98k 7.92mm bolt-action rifle with a five-round magazine. German designers adapted the same ammunition to an automatic weapon when they created the excellent MG34, giving the infantry squad its own

Panzergrenadiers run to catch up with an SdKfz 251 halftrack on the way out of a Russian village. German mechanized and motorized infantry rode to battle, but fought dismounted. (HITM)

With the Sturmgeschütz armored assault gun the Germans realized the Napoleonic dream of having artillery able to accompany infantry in the attack. Here a group of pioneers hitch a ride on a StuG III near Minsk on July 17. (NARA)

general purpose machine gun. After the western campaign many squad leaders carried 9mm MP38 and MP40 machine-pistols.

According to S.J. Lewis, the "better" infantry divisions were those of the earlier mobilization "waves": 1st Wave (26 divisions), 2nd (16), 4th (14), 5th (4), and 7th & 8th (24). Infantry leaders had suggested many improvements based on their experiences in Poland and France, but few were implemented in time for *Barbarossa*.

Artillery

The German artillery branch expanded from seven regiments in 1927 to over 100 in 1940. During that period it concentrated on rapid movement, rapid fire control adjustment and combined-arms operations. Their light and heavy field howitzers served as the backbone of divisional artillery throughout World War II.

Luftwaffe

Führer Directive 21 gave the Luftwaffe three concurrent missions: to defend Germany and her allies; to continue the war against England and her shipping; and to attack the Soviet Union. Its strength was thus dissipated over the continent of Europe (and soon, North Africa) while it was trying to rule the skies over the world's largest country. It employed many obsolete aircraft that were considered good enough to confront the even less modern equipment of the Red Army Air Force. No less than half of its transport aircraft had been lost on Crete immediately prior to *Barbarossa*. Despite the efforts of Von Richthofen and others, German air-ground co-ordination was still rudimentary. In fact, his elite VIII Fliegerkorps had to move from Greece and Yogoslavia to Suwalki between June 7 and 21, so 600 of its vehicles and 40 percent of its aircraft were unavailable on *Barbarossatag*. At its peak the VIII Fliegerkorps consisted of 87 twin-engine level bombers, 50 Junkers Ju 87B Stuka monoplane and 26 Henschel Hs 123 biplane dive-bombers, 22 Messerschmitt Bf 110 twin-engine fighters, and 66 Bf 109 single-engine fighters. The same miserable weather with which the army had to contend created boggy airfields and retarded the forward movement of maintenance, supply and communications assets.

Waffen-SS

The SS-Division "Reich" began as a collection of SS-Standarten (regiments) during the Polish campaign. These were united as the SS-Verfügungs

Division for France, then renamed "Reich" on February 25 1941. During *Barbarossa*, "Reich" was a motorized division made up of three motorized infantry regiments, an artillery regiment, and more than the usual number of assigned battalions.

In addition to this "armed SS" formation, security units such as Einsatzgruppe B and Polizei units under SS command followed close behind the Army Group to pursue the Nazis' policies of summary execution on racial and political grounds.

Austria

Numerous Wehrmacht units had Austrian origins and Austrian personnel. On April 1, 1936 Austria had thrown off the post-World War I Treaty of St Germain and instituted its own universal military service laws. Its forces grew from barely 20,000 men in six brigades to over 60,000 in seven infantry and one fast/mobile division plus two aviation regiments by the time of the Anschluss with Germany in March 1938. Its Bundesheer officially became part of the Wehrmacht on April 1, 1938.

* * *

Two special formations deserve mention:

Infantry Regiment "Grossdeutschland" (GD) This elite army formation began as a Berlin guard company with ceremonial duties; by the war's end it had grown into a complete mechanized corps. Its name, "Greater Germany," indicated that its soldiers were chosen from all over the country rather than from a specific Wehrkreis as with the rest of the army. In 1941 it was much stronger than its official designation suggested; "GD" had three infantry battalions, each with three line companies, a machine-gun company and a heavy company. A fourth battalion grouped a light infantry gun, an antitank, a heavy infantry gun and an assault gun company; reconnaissance, pioneer, signal and Flak companies made up the 5th Bn; and the regiment also had an artillery battalion and a logistics column.

Lehr Brigade (Motorized) 900 In order to keep army branch-of-service schools current with developments in the field, instructors needed combat experience; so the Replacement Army commander agreed to requests from these schools to create a unit to participate in *Barbarossa*, so long as this did not compromise their primary instruction mission. The brigade's organization was unsatisfactory, since the impact on the schools outweighed the need to create an efficient fighting unit. Lehr Bde (mot) 900 consisted of a headquarters, two battalions from the Döberitz Infantry School, one each Panzer (using captured French tanks) and antitank battalions from the Wünsdorf Panzer School, an artillery battalion and an assault gun battery from the Jüterbog Artillery School, plus medical and logistics support. Its supposed three-month deployment in fact lasted until March 1942, by which time it had been worn down to two companies and a few heavy weapons.

Occupation policies

The Soviet Union's own brutal 21-month occupation of eastern Poland and western Belorussia prior to June 1941 caused many inhabitants to welcome the Wehrmacht; Nazi concepts on the relative value of human lives soon put an end to such naive notions. Despite a German experiment with reformed occupation policies from October 1942 until June 1943, the main outcomes of Hitler's racial obsessions were a vengeful populace, a new legitimacy for Stalin and Communism, the tying down of a huge and wasteful occupation force, and ultimately, shame for the German nation.

THE RED ARMY

Force structure

The Soviet Union was born in war, and was in crisis, at war or preparing for war for most of its existence. By 1941 it was a garrison state: if the USSR were to survive, internal security had to be the first priority. Stalin's notorious purges lasted from 1937 right up to *Barbarossatag*; among their first and most famous victims was Marshal M.N. Tukhachevsky, who was persecuted on the basis of trumped-up evidence known to have originated with the Gestapo. These purges certainly weakened the senior Soviet military and administrative leadership; but new scholarship shows that this NKVD *Ezhovshchina* had less impact than earlier thought. Slightly more than 8 percent of Red Army officers were purged in 1938 (the worst year) – far short of the 30–50 percent previously quoted. Massive Soviet military expansion, especially following 1938, had far more impact on the decline of the army's quality. The Red Army added 111 rifle divisions, 12 rifle brigades plus 50 tank and motorized divisions between January 1939 and May 1941, its personnel strength growing from 1,500,000 to more than 5 million. During that period the proportion of officers attending required schooling plummeted, course length shrank from 36 to 24 months and later to 18 months, and the rank of instructors fell from major or captain to senior lieutenant.

Fatefully, the Soviets made a conscious decision to field more partial-strength formations rather than fewer full-strength ones. This sent many field-grade officers and generals to the staffs of additional division and corps headquarters rather than retaining quality leadership at the lower levels. The infantry, which would do most of the fighting in any future war, also gave up many of its junior officers to other branches such as tank troops, the Air Force and NKVD security units.

Furthermore, on the eve of *Barbarossa* the 170 divisions in the western USSR were short of 1,500,000 men. Even if all 800,000 soldiers mobilized in the spring of 1941 had gone to these units they would have made up only half the shortfall; in fact, half of those mobilized went to the Air Force, and to units deep in the interior of the USSR. Combined, these factors meant that at the critical point of attack the Red Army was missing essential leadership at the battalion and regiment level, and was understrength everywhere.

National leadership

Despite the dictator's supposed leadership experiences gained during the Russian Civil War, Zhukov considered Stalin strictly a military dilettante. Especially during the early stages of the Nazi–Soviet War he interfered in military decisions with disastrous results. Unlike Hitler, however, Stalin learned to trust his professional experts as the war progressed. Quite apart from the manifest failures of the Czarist army, Soviet theorists blamed Russia's collapse during World War I on three other factors: the incompetence or outright rebellion of the peasantry, bureaucracy, and railroads. Uncompromising Communist Party leadership rectified these issues, and took pains to eliminate earlier "isolated caste relations," so no alternative to Stalin's state arose during the Great Patriotic War.

The psychological damage of the purges was perhaps greater than the material. It is often said that fear stifled the initiative of field commanders; as significant is the fact that the purges caused a widespread lack of trust in the Soviet leadership and a diminished faith in the institutions of the state. Soldiers might wonder why it had taken Stalin so long to uncover the "traitors"; and, if the rank and file could not trust stalwarts such as Tukhachevsky, whom could they trust?

New commanders came to the fore in mid-1940 following the debacle in Finland. Marshals S.K. Timoshenko and B.M. Shaposhnikov took over as Defense Commissar and Deputy/Chief of Staff respectively. They, and Zhukov from January of the next year, tried but failed to reform the Soviet military after decades of chaos bordering on negligence. Entrenched conservatives (as everywhere) challenged the efforts of the reformers, as did the NKVD. Like Germany, the USSR suffered from a lack of strategic thinking. At a three-week meeting of the Main Military Council held immediately before the famous December–January wargames, most participants concentrated on the tactical lessons of the Spanish Civil War, Khalkin Gol and the Winter War; it seems that only Timoshenko thought primarily of strategy and a possible war against Hitler.

A Soviet described in the German caption as a divisional political officer ("commissar") is interrogated by his captors, although the red star forearm badge of that status is not visible in this print. If he is a commissar then his life expectancy is now minimal; Hitler issued express orders that such prisoners were to be executed. (Author's collection)

Doctrine

Writings in the 1920s had voiced fuzzy theories about a "proletarian" way of war; but, even in 1939, a Field Regulation boasted that the "invincible, all shattering Red Army" would take war to the enemy and "achieve decisive victory with little blood" – an emphasis carried over to the next year's edition. As discussed in the earlier volumes of this trilogy, Soviet doctrine was essentially offensive: after a defensive along their borderlands, the Red Army would attack into the enemy's home territory. Even after the fall of France, Soviet leaders – ignoring both the lessons of Blitzkrieg and their own maneuver doctrine – thought in anachronistic terms of a lengthy border battle followed by breakthrough operations. The assumption that the Red Army would have time to mobilize before launching its counter-offensive stands out as a critical failure of the October 1940 and May 1941 State Defense Plans. The Red Army gave little thought to the defense, and so had no shield behind which to prepare. They also failed completely to anticipate the nature of a potential German attack; after the war, Zhukov wrote that neither he, Timoshenko nor Shaposhnikov "calculated that the enemy would concentrate such a mass of armored and motorized forces and hurl them in compact groups on all strategic axes on the first day."

The Soviet soldier

Despite conventional wisdom that Red Army soldiers possessed natural fieldcraft skills, the Soviet campaigns of 1939–40 revealed a poor grasp of personal camouflage, entrenching, river-crossing and other basic tasks. Officers could not read maps, and displayed both drunkenness and *naprasnoi smelosti* (futile bravery). All were too prone to panic when confronted with opposition, as happened in Poland. Excessive secrecy, which pervaded all of Soviet society, meant that leaders and soldiers at all levels were surprised by battlefield situations and conditions, and therefore less able to adapt. (One week into *Barbarossa*, rumors ran rampant that Budenny had taken Warsaw and Voroshilov was advancing on Berlin!)

The purges had caused a decline in respect for all officers. This attitude applied to a purged officer's replacement, and even to those officers who were quickly reinstated (one-third of the total). Discipline was universally poor, with what was called *shapkozkidatel'stvo* (hat tossing) symptomatic of the malaise. The transfer of too many field-grade officers to higher headquarters contributed to this weakness, and one report described the loose relations between company-grade officers and their men as "pseudo democratic." The system then in place had no formalized rewards or punishments. Timoshenko implemented changes in summer 1940, but nearly a year later inspections of units reported frustratingly little progress. *Barbarossa* would expose these weaknesses all too clearly.

Fortifications

An integral part of the shield behind which the Soviets would prepare for their strategic counteroffensives were their Fortified Regions. Called the "Stalin Line" by the Germans, they were in no way comparable to the Maginot Line; the main works consisted of bunkers with light artillery and machine guns. One of the two oldest Fortified Regions was that at Polotsk astride the River Dvina, where the Soviet, Polish and Lithuanian borders came together. Others, at Minsk, Mozyr and Slutsk, dated from the 1930s.

A temporary transfer of power in Belorussia: on July 10, German troops pass the Minsk "House of Soviets" with its statue of Lenin. (NARA)

A favored weapon since the Russian Civil War, the armored train proved to be a useful tool given the huge distances and poor roads in the Soviet Union. This example mounts T-34/76 tank turrets. (Courtesy of the Central Museum of the Armed Forces Moscow)

Stalin insisted that the defensive lines move west into Poland in 1939. In June 1940, a month after replacing Voroshilov, Timoshenko ordered new construction in these areas, including updating Fortress Brest's defenses. On *Barbarossatag* most divisions manning the Soviet–German frontier lacked their engineer battalions which were busy building new bunkers and obstacles, markedly degrading the divisions' combat power. Construction went slowly, partially owing to the same miserable transportation infrastructure that would soon hamstring Von Bock's advance. Prior to *Barbarossa*, Red Army inspectors found the Minsk defenses "deplorable." The German after-action report claimed that only 193 of the 1,175 forts throughout the West Front area were equipped and occupied.

Guards divisions

In a bow to Imperial tradition, the Red Army reintroduced the honorific title of "Guards" for divisions (and later corps and armies) that excelled on the battlefield. Following the battles of Smolensk, on September 18 it created the first four when the 100th, 127th, 153rd and 161st Rifle Divisions became the 1st, 2nd, 3rd and 4th Guards Rifle Divisions (the first-named already had elite status as the "Order of Lenin Division", established in 1923). Initially the only benefit of the new title was a boost to morale; however, later in the war Guards organizations received greater numbers of above-average personnel and equipment.

Red Army Air Force

Following the campaigns against Japan and Finland the Air Force labored under a false sense of superiority compared to the Army. In reality, much of its equipment was obsolescent and worn out. It also had weak antiaircraft artillery, no protected parking, and limited temporary airfields to which aircraft could disperse when threatened. Only senior leaders carried radios, maps and target information in their aircraft. The Air Force did have some advantages over the Luftwaffe, however: the benefits in sub-zero temperatures enjoyed by the air-cooled engines of some Soviet fighters over the water-cooled Messerschmitts were obvious. The Air Force's mission under the 1936 regulations was limited to close air support; the USSR gave up on strategic bombing in the late 1930s, when it disbanded its three strategic air armies and canceled the four-engine TB-7 bomber.

Unlike their relatively unprepared German counterparts, these warmly dressed and camouflaged Soviet troops – the two-man crew of one of the Red Army's ubiquitous Maxim M1910 machine guns – are well equipped for fighting in the snow. (From the fonds of the RGAKFD at Krasnogorsk)

The battlefield

Belorussia has no natural frontiers, and for centuries the native population had resisted Mongol, Kievan, Lithuanian, Polish, Russian, German and Soviet masters. The theater of war covered here literally and figuratively divided the western USSR. To the north lies the lake district, where Scandinavian ice sheets had scoured out the thin layer of earth; to the south are the Rokitno Marshes and other poorly drained areas. In between, marking the farthest advance of the glaciers, lay deposits that created the drainage divide along the line Grodno–Minsk–Smolensk–Valdai Hills. The contemporary highway and rail lines followed this traditional commercial and invasion route (called the Post Road in Napoleonic times). Parallel routes ran from Latvia through Vitebsk and Rzhev (in 1941, Hoth's area), and from Brest through Gomel and Bryansk (Guderian's area).

The Desna, Dnepr, Dvina, Moscow and Volga rivers all have their sources in this high gound. The "River Gate" represented the ridgeline's crowning feature – basically the relative high ground (in reality, only approximately 600 feet in elevation) – between Vitebsk and Orsha and centered on Smolensk. Hoth describes this feature as being approximately 42 miles wide: enough room for three armored divisions to maneuver. The lobe pattern representing the glacier's margin also had military significance – for example, in the northward jut of the Berezina river.

A Red Army artillery firing position in the winter. During *Barbarossa*, Soviet artillery did not yet play the decisive and dominating role that it later would. During the summer and autumn of 1941 Zhukov husbanded his artillery for the battle that he knew would develop around Moscow. (Elukka)

ORDERS OF BATTLE

GERMAN

ARMY GROUP CENTER[3] – GFM Fedor von Bock
OKH Reserve:
Higher Command XXXV – Gen Kav R. Koch-Erpach
15 Inf Div – GenLt E-E. Hell (from July 3)
52 Inf Div – GenMaj L. Rendulic (from June 26)
106 Inf Div – GenMaj E. Dehmer (from July 1)
110 Inf Div – GenLt E. Seifert (from June 26)
112 Inf Div – Gen Inf F. Mieth (from July 1)
197 Inf Div – GenLt H. Meyer-Rabingen (from June 26)
Lehr Bde (mot) 900 – Obst W. Krause (from June 22)
Army Group Reserve:
293 Inf Div – GenLt J. von Obernitz

Third Panzer Group – GenObst H. Hoth
XXXIX Panzer Corps – Gen PzTr R. Schmidt
7 Pz Div – GenMaj H. von Funck
20 Pz Div – GenMaj H. Stumpff
14 Mot Inf Div – GenLt F. Fuerst
20 Mot Inf Div – GenMaj H. Zorn

LVII Panzer Corps – Gen PzTr A. Kuntzen
12 Pz Div – GenMaj J. Harpe
19 Pz Div – GenLt O. von Knoblesdorff
18 Mot Inf Div – GenMaj F. Herrlein

V Army Corps – Gen Inf R. Ruoff
5 Inf Div – GenMaj K. Allmendinger
35 Inf Div – GenLt W. von Weikersthal

VI Army Corps – Gen Pi O-W. Foerster
6 Inf Div – GenLt H. Auleb
26 Inf Div – GenMaj W. Weiss

Ninth Army – GenObst A. Strauss
VIII Army Corps – Gen Art W. Heitz
8 Inf Div – GenMaj G. Hoehne
28 Inf Div – GenLt J. Sinnhuber
161 Ind Div – GenLt H. Wilck

XX Army Corps – Gen Inf W. Materna
162 Inf Div – GenLt H. Franke
256 Inf Div – GenLt G. Kauffmann

XLII Army Corps – Gen Pi W. Kuntze
87 Inf Div – GenLt B. von Studnitz
102 Inf Div – GenLt J. Ansat
129 Inf Div – GenMaj S. Rittau

Fourth Army – GFM Günther Hans von Kluge
VII Army Corps – Gen Art W. Fahrmbacher
7 Inf Div – GenLt E. von Gablenz
23 Inf Div – GenMaj H. Hellmich
258 Inf Div – GenMaj W. Henrici
268 Inf Div – GenLt E. Straube

XIII Army Corps – Gen Inf H. Felber
17 Inf Div – GenLt H. Loch
78 Inf Div – GenLt C. Gallenkamp

IX Army Corps – Gen Inf H. Geyer
137 Inf Div – GenLt H. Kamencke
263 Inf Div – GenLt F. Karl
292 Inf Div – GenLt M. Dehmel

XLII Army Corps – Gen Inf G. Heinrici
131 Inf Div – GenLt H. Meyer-Buerdorff
134 Inf Div – GenLt C. von Cochenhausen
252 Inf Div – GenLt D. von Boehm-Benzing

Second Panzer Group – GenObst H. Guderian
Reserve:
255 Inf Div – Gen Inf W. Wetzel

XXIV Panzer Corps – Gen PzTr L. Geyr von Schweppenburg
3 Pz Div – GenLt W. Model
4 Pz Div – GenMaj W. von Langermann
10 Mot Inf Div – GenLt F-W. von Loeper
1 Cav Div – GenLt O. Mengers
267 Inf Div – GenMaj R. Martinek

XLVI Panzer Corps – Gen PzTr H. von Vietinghoff
10 Pz Div – GenLt F. Schaal
Inf Regt "Grossdeutschland" – Obst W-H. von Stockenhausen
SS "Reich" – SS-Ogruf P. Hausser

XLVII Panzer Corps – Gen PzTr J. Lemelsen
17 Pz Div – GenLt H-J. von Arnim
18 Pz Div – GenMaj W. Nehring
29 Mot Inf Div – GenMaj W. von Boltenstern
167 Inf Div – GenLt H. Schoenhaerl

XII Army Corps – Gen Inf W. Schroth
31 Inf Div – GenMaj G. Berthold
34 Inf Div – GenLt H. Behrendorff
45 Inf Div – GenMaj F. Schlieper

Rear Army Area 102 – GenLt M. von Schenkendorff
221 Security Div – GenLt J. Pflugbeil
286 Security Div – GenLt K. Mueller
403 Security Div – GenLt W. Ditfurth

---

3 No two sources on orders of battle for *Barbarossa* agree. The primary source used here is Horst Boog (ed.), *Germany and the Second World War.*

SOVIET

WEST FRONT[4] – Colonel-General D.G. Pavlov
Front units:
2nd Rifle Corps – MajGen A.N. Ermakov
100th Rifle Division
161st Rifle Division

21st Rifle Corps – MajGen V.B. Borisov
17th Rifle Division
24th Rifle Division
37th Rifle Division

44th Rifle Corps – MajGen V.A. Yushkevich
64th Rifle Division
108th Rifle Division

47th Rifle Corps – MajGen S.I. Povetkin
50th Rifle Division
55th Rifle Division
121st Rifle Division
143rd Rifle Division

4th Airborne Corps – MajGen A.S. Zhandov
7th, 8th & 214th Airborne Brigades
8th Antitank Brigade

17th Mechanized Corps – MajGen M.P. Petrov
27th Tank Division
36th Tank Division
209th Motorized Division
22nd Motorcycle Regiment

20th Mechanized Corps – MajGen A.G. Nikitin
26th Tank Division
38th Tank Division
210th Motorized Division
24th Motorcycle Regiment

3rd Army – LtGen V.I. Kuznetsov
4th Rifle Corps
27th Rifle Division
56th Rifle Division
85th Rifle Division

11th Mechanized Corps – MajGen D.K. Mostevenko
29th Tank Division
33rd Tank Division
204th Motorized Division
16th Motorcycle Regiment
7th Antitank Brigade

4th Army – MajGen A.A. Korobkov
28th Rifle Corps – MajGen V.S. Popov
6th Rifle Division
42nd Rifle Division
49th Rifle Division
75th Rifle Division

14th Mechanized Corps – MajGen S.I. Oborin
22nd Tank Division
30th Tank Division
205th Motorized Division
20th Motorcycle Regiment

10th Army – MajGen K.D. Golubev
1st Rifle Corps – MajGen F.D. Rubtsev
2nd Rifle Division
8th Rifle Division

5th Rifle Corps – MajGen A.V. Garnov
13th Rifle Division
86th Rifle Division
113th Rifle Division

6th Cavalry Corps – MajGen I.S. Nikitin
6th Cavalry Division
36th Cavalry Division
6th Antitank Brigade

6th Mechanized Corps – MajGen M.G. Khatskilevich
4th Tank Division
7th Tank Division
29th Motorized Division
4th Motorcycle Regiment

13th Mechanized Corps – MajGen P.N. Akhliustin
25th Tank Division
31st Tank Division
208th Motorized Division
18th Motorcycle Regiment

---

4 As with the German order of battle, the sources conflict on the details of Red Army organization. The primary source used here is David Glantz, *Barbarossa*.

OPERATION *BARBAROSSA*

FRONTIER BATTLES – THE FIRST FORTNIGHT

By May 30, German units in occupied Poland learned of their change of mission: they were no longer on the defensive, but were preparing to invade the USSR. Headquarters of all echelons completed preparations; new units arrived constantly from the Reich, France and the Balkans, some rolling off rail cars to their final assembly areas even after June 22. Besides practicing and checking equipment, some soldiers marked their final days of occupation duty with soccer games and unit equestrian competitions. The Ostheer waited for the unusually high, fast-flowing rivers to subside. During the night of June 20–21, Von Bock's men moved their heavy weapons forward. The next night was dark with only a faint crescent of the waning moon. Austrians of the 137th Infantry Division watched their Soviet counterparts across the border working to improve their positions under illumination provided by vehicle headlights. In Minsk, Gen Pavlov returned from the theater, but was kept from his bed by reports of increased German activity. Sunrise came at 0410hrs on that Sunday of June 22, but by that time *Barbarossa* was already an hour old.

Breakthrough

After numerous requests, Timoshenko finally allowed Pavlov to alert his troops at 0300hrs, but this was generally a futile gesture. The Ninth Army and Third Panzer Group attacked at 0305hrs in co-ordination with Army Group North, while Fourth Army and Second Panzer Group moved out at 0315hrs, as did Von Rundstedt to their south. As the mission and enemy situation dictated, certain units enjoyed massive artillery preparatory fire while others did without.

In some places along the River Bug, Guderian's men captured bridges intact by ruse; elsewhere they used assault boats, covered by Sturmgeschütz fire, to force their way across. In the 18th Panzer Division sector, 80 specially modified "submarine" tanks of I/Panzer Regiment 18 waded across under water. Hoth's men faced a "dry" front, but would encounter three rivers within a little over 40 miles of the frontier. In the former Soviet zone many Polish peasants naively greeted the Germans with salt and bread, their traditional gifts to travelers.

Pavlov's men offered little or no resistance for hours. Since mid-June he had been asking in vain for permission to occupy forward positions. Timoshenko telephoned on June 22 to tell Pavlov's deputy Boldin, "No action is to be taken against the Germans without our knowledge... Tell Pavlov that Comrade Stalin has forbidden artillery fire against the Germans." Pavlov meekly concluded that "some kind of devilry" by German "provocationists" must be going on.

Army Group Center had to fight its way across many watercourses. Here a Horch staff car crosses a river on a ferry made by lashing together inflatable rafts overlaid with timbers and powered by an assault boat. (HITM)

At 0200hrs on June 22, West Front air commander Colonel I.I. Kopets reported to Pavlov that his forces were at full readiness. By nightfall he had lost 738 aircraft – 40 percent of his strength; he would commit suicide shortly afterward. His pilots essentially did the same, flying hopeless counterattacks.

German radio intercepts overheard Soviet transmissions asking, "The Germans are attacking, what should I do?" Third Panzer Group tanks captured all three essential bridges on their assault axis before the Soviet engineers could blow the demolition charges. Two thousand vehicles of VIII Fliegerkorps intermingled with Hoth's armor on the few decent roads; they were his biggest headache – until 7th Panzer Division encountered 5th Tank Division's hull-down T-34s guarding the east bank of the 150-yard-wide Neman river. A day later the 5th numbered only 15 functioning tanks, and XXXIX Panzer Corps was marching on. Operationally, Hoth pulled off a major coup by splitting the boundary between the Northwest and West Fronts.

By 1500hrs Guderian's 3rd Panzer Division, followed by the 4th, had worked their way around the fortress of Brest, and into the open country near Kobrin. No sooner did the Germans cross the border than they hit sandy terrain that multiplied their fuel consumption; they also learned quickly that the Soviets fought better in the woods than they did.

Pavlov had no idea of conditions at the front, but nevertheless went about issuing attack orders to imaginary "shock groups." Although his 3rd and 4th Armies began to fall back, the 10th remained close to the border. German ground and air attacks had scattered the headquarters of both 3rd and 4th Armies; Kuznetsov at the 3rd managed to send one signal that entire day – "We are through." Meanwhile Pavlov sent his deputy Boldin to the command post of the 10th to assess the situation. In fact, 10th Army commander Golubev had already ordered his 13th Mechanized Corps to counterattack. Zhukov and the high command knew less about the front than Pavlov, and what they did know paled in comparison to the reality. In many cases Moscow depended on local Party officials to confirm army information. Conflicting stories describe Stalin as suffering a nervous breakdown and disappearing from the Kremlin for the remainder of June. However, the historian David Murphy has written that only at 1300hrs that terrible Sunday did Stalin "begin to act as a commander." He dispatched Chief of Staff Shaposhnikov to the West Front headquarters – a useless gesture, given the chaos and misinformation that reigned there.

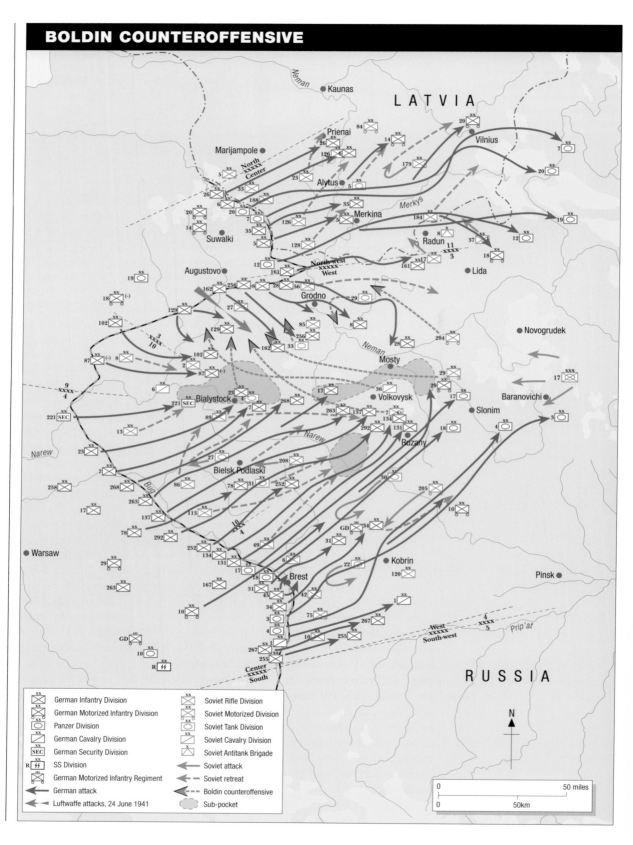

Legend:

- German Infantry Division
- German Motorized Infantry Division
- Panzer Division
- German Cavalry Division
- German Security Division
- SS Division
- German Motorized Infantry Regiment
- German attack
- Luftwaffe attacks, 24 June 1941
- Soviet Rifle Division
- Soviet Motorized Division
- Soviet Tank Division
- Soviet Cavalry Division
- Soviet Antitank Brigade
- Soviet attack
- Soviet retreat
- Boldin counteroffensive
- Sub-pocket

The world's most technologically advanced tank squandered in a bog: behind a knocked-out T-26, three T-34s are stuck where incompetent crews drove them. The T-34 was the world's best tank until the arrival of the German PzKpfw V Panther in 1943. (Author's collection)

Within 24 hours Hoth had broken through the main defensive belt, and Von Bock rewarded his achieving operational freedom by releasing Third Panzer Group from Ninth Army control. All did not go well on the 23rd, however. The 20th Panzer Division, which had been competing with 7th Panzer for the same road, had to delay its attack on Vilnius because of a lack of fuel; this did not bode well for *Barbarossa*. Also that day, the Red Army Air Force made a feeble ten-plane bombing raid on Königsberg in accordance with the USSR's "Red Folder" prewar offensive plans.

Pavlov, too, was trying to launch counterattacks as demanded by naive instructions to "use all measures to defend Grodno." But 8th Infantry Division continued to pound that town with 29 batteries of artillery. Hoth's advance widened the gap between 3rd and 11th Armies to nearly 100 miles. Pavlov still had virtually no communications with, and so little control over his field armies. In any event, they were in no position to launch the called-for counteroffensive. Pavlov therefore sent Boldin to assemble an attack force and move on Grodno, theoretically to threaten Hoth's southern flank and restore the situation.

Von Bock's reported advance looked incredible from Rastenburg, and by the second day of *Barbarossa* German plans were already beginning to

fray. First, Hitler wanted to halt the armor in order to eliminate the developing Bialystok pocket. Halder at OKH resolutely fought this idea, and ordered Von Bock to create inner infantry and outer armored encirclements before Minsk. Von Bock protested this interference, but ultimately obeyed orders. Finally Von Brauchitsch intervened, and allowed Von Bock to send Hoth's "reconnaissance in force" toward Vitebsk and Polotsk, while Guderian made for Slutsk, Bobruisk and Rogatchev. Thus, less than 48 hours into the campaign, the dispersal of the Army Group's tank forces began – tactically prudent, but operationally fatal. A lack of consensus between the supreme warlord, the army commander-in-chief, his chief of staff and the field generals was already developing.

Boldin's counterattack

As would be the case throughout *Barbarossa*, the contradictions at the strategic level did not equate to inactivity farther down the chain of command. Hoth's tanks were advancing at a tremendous rate and already threatened Minsk from the north. Following Pavlov's orders, Boldin's "shock group" – basically 6th (with over 1,000 tanks) and 11th Mechanized and the 6th Cavalry Corps – advanced toward Grodno in a counterclockwise arc with an ultimate objective of Augustovo. Luftwaffe reconnaissance had been looking deep in the Soviet rear and missed this build-up, so Boldin initially surprised Strauss. (He missed Hoth, his primary target, who was already long gone.)

In common with Soviet attacks all along the front during those early days, Boldin's suffered from poor command and control, no effective air support, weak combined-arms tactics and insufficient logistics. Approximately half of the 6th Mechanized Corps' tanks were modern T-34s and KVs, but these had only been received a month earlier, so the crews were unfamiliar with them. A Luftwaffe attack on 6th Cavalry Corps destroyed 70 percent of its 36th Cavalry Division in 24 hours. Boldin's assault created a small crisis among the German 256th Infantry Division around Grodno, but could not distract Third Panzer Group. Since these early battles were meeting engagements, they all heavily favored the more experienced Germans.

On the southern side of the bulge, Guderian's tanks neared Baranovichi. The 22nd Tank Division, attempting to bar the way of the 3rd and 18th Panzer Divisions, lost its commanding general. The 14th Mechanized Corps counted 478 operational tanks on June 22, but against Guderian's veterans that number shrank to 250 two days later, and to only 30 on the 26th, by which time Hoth already threatened Minsk.

Pavlov's counterattacks had shot their bolt by June 25, one mile shy of Grodno's center, low on fuel and ammunition and with little to show. The 11th Mechanized Corps lost all but 30 of its 305 tanks, and melted away from 32,000 men to 600 in four days. Caught behind enemy lines near the western edge of the front, Boldin and about 2,000 of his men began a 45-day evasion that would eventually lead them to freedom east of Smolensk.

On that day, Timoshenko instructed the West Front to withdraw to the Lida–Slonim–Pinsk line. Pavlov tried to establish an additional defensive position slightly to the north near Radun, with 21st Rifle Corps supported by 8th Antitank Brigade, but these maneuvers had already been overcome by events.

Completing the Minsk encirclements

Fortress Brest still held out despite the pounding of 210mm howitzers, two 600mm siege guns and Nebelwerfer rockets. The Bialystok salient had been custom-made for a huge *Kessel*, a weakness Hitler and OKH wanted to exploit as quickly as possible. Von Bock was already thinking past that, but higher headquarters still thought in terms of exterminating Red Army units before reaching the Dnepr, so Army Group Center slowly began to squeeze the life out of Pavlov's West Front as ordered.

In Moscow, on June 25 the newly formed Stavka (High Command Committee) ordered a 1st Cavalry Army crony of Stalin's, Marshal S.M. Budenny, to create the Reserve Front using 19th, 20th, 21st and 22nd Armies, on exactly the same Vitebsk–Orsha line for which Von Bock aimed. Luftwaffe reconnaissance noticed this development beginning to take shape on July 1. In Stalin's study a day later, Zhukov drew two arcs on a map where 24th and 28th Armies (13 rifle, six tank and three

Terrain in the Third Panzer Group's area was more thickly forested than farther south in the Second Panzer Group sector. These vehicles bear the "Hh" of Hoth's formation, plus the yellow Y-rune of the famous 7th Panzer Division – one of several whose tank regiment was still equipped with the Czechoslovak-made PzKpfw 35(t) or 38(t). (Podzun)

MINSK ENCIRCLEMENT

After the initial border battles the Second and Third Panzer Groups raced east past Minsk and on 27 June slammed the door shut on Army Group Center's first *Kessel*. Actually a number of smaller encirclements, the Minsk pocket meant the Western Front's initial defense lasted only two weeks.

Note: Gridlines are shown at intervals of 50km/31miles

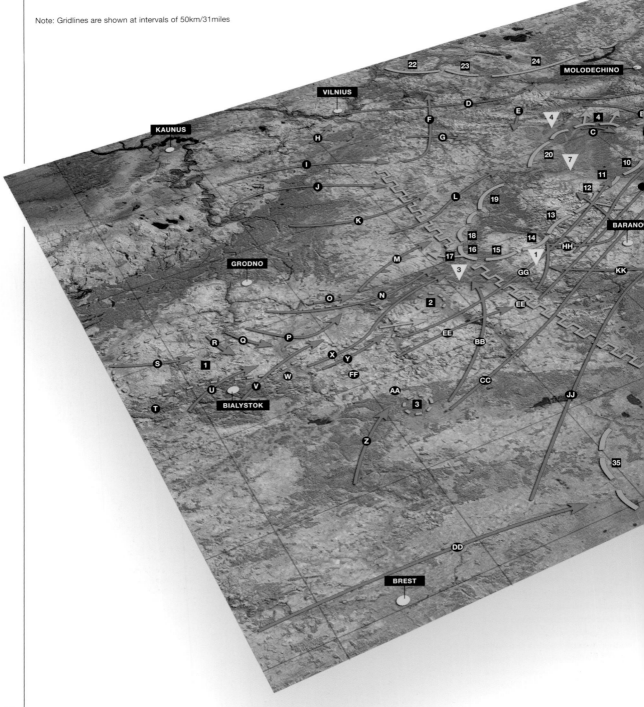

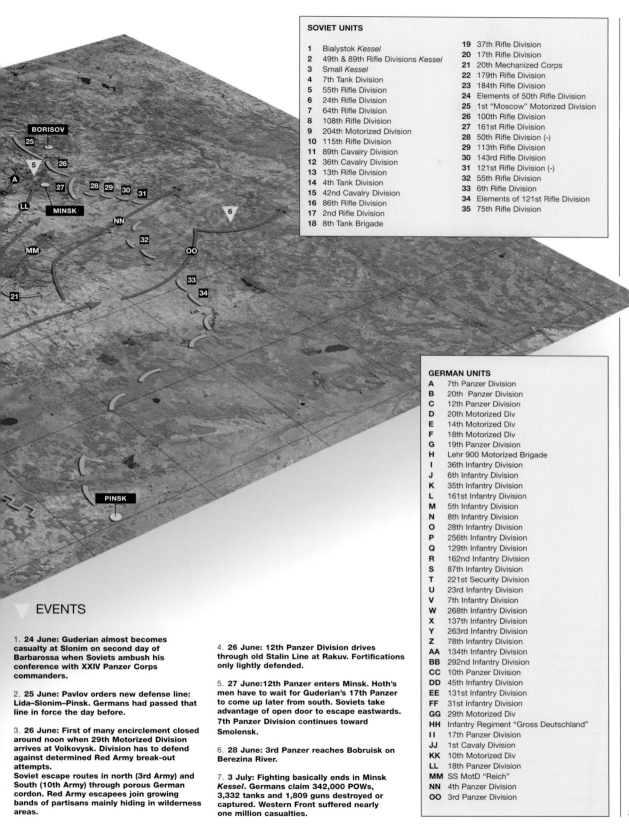

SOVIET UNITS

1	Bialystok *Kessel*
2	49th & 89th Rifle Divisions *Kessel*
3	Small *Kessel*
4	7th Tank Division
5	55th Rifle Division
6	24th Rifle Division
7	64th Rifle Division
8	108th Rifle Division
9	204th Motorized Division
10	115th Rifle Division
11	89th Cavalry Division
12	36th Cavalry Division
13	13th Rifle Division
14	4th Tank Division
15	42nd Cavalry Division
16	86th Rifle Division
17	2nd Rifle Division
18	8th Tank Brigade
19	37th Rifle Division
20	17th Rifle Division
21	20th Mechanized Corps
22	179th Rifle Division
23	184th Rifle Division
24	Elements of 50th Rifle Division
25	1st "Moscow" Motorized Division
26	100th Rifle Division
27	161st Rifle Division
28	50th Rifle Division (-)
29	113th Rifle Division
30	143rd Rifle Division
31	121st Rifle Division (-)
32	55th Rifle Division
33	6th Rifle Division
34	Elements of 121st Rifle Division
35	75th Rifle Division

GERMAN UNITS

A	7th Panzer Division
B	20th Panzer Division
C	12th Panzer Division
D	20th Motorized Div
E	14th Motorized Div
F	18th Motorized Div
G	19th Panzer Division
H	Lehr 900 Motorized Brigade
I	36th Infantry Division
J	6th Infantry Division
K	35th Infantry Division
L	161st Infantry Division
M	5th Infantry Division
N	8th Infantry Division
O	28th Infantry Division
P	256th Infantry Division
Q	129th Infantry Division
R	162nd Infantry Division
S	87th Infantry Division
T	221st Security Division
U	23rd Infantry Division
V	7th Infantry Division
W	268th Infantry Division
X	137th Infantry Division
Y	263rd Infantry Division
Z	78th Infantry Division
AA	134th Infantry Division
BB	292nd Infantry Division
CC	10th Panzer Division
DD	45th Infantry Division
EE	131st Infantry Division
FF	31st Infantry Division
GG	29th Motorized Div
HH	Infantry Regiment "Gross Deutschland"
II	17th Panzer Division
JJ	1st Cavaly Division
KK	10th Motorized Div
LL	18th Panzer Division
MM	SS MotD "Reich"
NN	4th Panzer Division
OO	3rd Panzer Division

▼ EVENTS

1. **24 June:** Guderian almost becomes casualty at Slonim on second day of Barbarossa when Soviets ambush his conference with XXIV Panzer Corps commanders.

2. **25 June:** Pavlov orders new defense line: Lida–Slonim–Pinsk. Germans had passed that line in force the day before.

3. **26 June:** First of many encirclement closed around noon when 29th Motorized Division arrives at Volkovysk. Division has to defend against determined Red Army break-out attempts.
Soviet escape routes in north (3rd Army) and South (10th Army) through porous German cordon. Red Army escapees join growing bands of partisans mainly hiding in wilderness areas.

4. **26 June:** 12th Panzer Division drives through old Stalin Line at Rakuv. Fortifications only lightly defended.

5. **27 June:** 12th Panzer enters Minsk. Hoth's men have to wait for Guderian's 17th Panzer to come up later from south. Soviets take advantage of open door to escape eastwards. 7th Panzer Division continues toward Smolensk.

6. **28 June:** 3rd Panzer reaches Bobruisk on Berezina River.

7. **3 July:** Fighting basically ends in Minsk *Kessel*. Germans claim 342,000 POWs, 3,332 tanks and 1,809 guns destroyed or captured. Western Front suffered nearly one million casualties.

In 1941 the summer was as hot as the spring had been wet and the winter would be cold. Ironically, it was often hotter in the Army Group Center area of operations than in the south. Drinking water was a constant logistical concern. (HITM)

motorized divisions) would establish a second defensive line centered on Yelnia, and a third stretching from Viazma to Kaluga. The Red Army would soon begin to occupy row after row of defensive fortifications between Smolensk and Moscow.

On June 27, Zhukov ordered the embattled Pavlov: (1) to achieve positive control over front units; (2) not to abandon tanks and artillery; (3) to evacuate Minsk and Bobruisk; (4) to counterattack to separate the German armor from the slower infantry; and (5), to detach cavalry into the Rokitno Marshes to initiate partisan warfare. He did not clarify the apparently contradictory nature of items 3 and 4; and anyway, West Front forces were still too decisively engaged to withdraw.

Voroshilov now arrived at Pavlov's headquarters to prop up the West Front commander; "the main thing is to overcome the Panzer phobia," he advised. On that same day Shaposhnikov received captured German maps indicating that the *Schwerpunkt* lay in the direction of Moscow and not the Ukraine as previously assumed. A blind man could see what was about to happen to the West Front's entire first echelon, but the Chief of Staff dared not recommend a full-scale withdrawal that could have saved some of Pavlov's command – after all, Stalin was still thinking offensively.

On June 25, Von Kluge, unable to close the trap on Pavlov, took 29th Motorized Division away from a protesting Guderian to establish a blocking position at Volkovysk. The 29th held until June 29 against Soviet break-out attempts by cavalry, tanks and human-wave assaults four men deep. The division's position divided two of the three Minsk pockets – Bialystok to the west, and Novogrudek to the east. However, on the northern edge of the pocket Ninth Army and Third Panzer Group's hammer struck before Fourth Army or Second Panzer Group's anvil was in place to the south, thereby allowing many Soviets to escape to the southeast.

Climate and terrain assisted the Soviet defenders. Extreme heat dried up various watercourses; while this made fording easier for the advancing Germans, thirst, flies and mosquitoes tormented men and horses. With their armies no longer effective fighting forces, Red Army soldiers melted away into thick forests. The sandy soil slowed the Germans further; moving an artillery piece often required 12–16 horses. Commandeered Russian *panje* pony-wagons, and captured Soviet farm tractors used as artillery prime movers, added to the shabby, gypsy-caravan aspect of their

Colonel-General Heinz Guderian and subordinates at an impromptu commanders' conference. Usually leading from the front, the headstrong Guderian had to defend himself with his personal weapon to avoid capture on several occasions, including June 24. On the same day the future Field Marshal Walter Model, commanding 3rd Panzer Division, narrowly survived the destruction by gunfire of his armored vehicle. (HITM)

columns. After three days many trailing units of the lead corps still had yet to cross the old frontier, and the gap between them and the slashing Panzer divisions was widening daily.

More than 200 of Von Richthofen's aircraft had a field day destroying Boldin's stranded, often out-of-fuel tanks. The Bf 110, outclassed in air-to-air combat in the West, began to enjoy a new lease of life as a ground-attack aircraft. As soon as the armor captured Soviet airfields the fighter squadrons – led by battle-proven veterans of Spain, Poland, France and the Battle of Britain – began operating from them, against their usually inexperienced opponents. Nevertheless, within three days of the invasion the first of the formidable Il-2 *Sturmovik* ground-attack aircraft, fresh from the Voronezh factory, appeared in the Army Group Center sector.

Guderian raced east, seemingly oblivious to the German goal of closing encirclements; neither was "Fast Heinz" overly concerned with his personal safety – some of Korobkov's troops almost captured him on June 24. The 17th Panzer Division took Slonim from the 4th Army, uncovering the southern route to Minsk, but was in turn surrounded and had to be saved by its sister 18th Panzer.

On June 25, 19th Panzer's motorcycle battalion and its commanding general Otto von Knoblesdorff led Hoth's Third Panzer Group to Minsk. Guderian's advanced units closed on the flaming town of Slutsk, which two days later Pavlov would futilely order the 20th Mechanized and 4th Airborne Corps to recapture. The Second Panzer Group had now left Belorussia and entered into Russia. By the 28th, Von Kluge considered that Guderian had also achieved operational freedom, and cut him loose from Fourth Army control.

Hoth continued to exploit the widening wound in the Soviet defenses between the Northwest and West Fronts. He too would rather have headed due east than have to worry about closing encirclements, but Hoth was less blatant in his obstinacy than Guderian. His LVII Panzer Corps took Vilnius on the 24th, while XXXIX Panzer Corps drove on Minsk itself. That same day Pavlov ordered 13th Army – "a mishmash of troops" – to attack the latter. However, a day later the 13th evacuated Molodechno, opening the way to Minsk for the ever-opportunistic 7th Panzer Division. Reflecting the continuing confusion resulting from Zhukov's instructions that day, Pavlov ordered General Filatov of 13th Army to stand fast. Meanwhile, Hoth received Lehr Brigade 900 to reinforce his over-extended Panzer group.

Beyond Minsk

Third Panzer Group broke through the "Stalin Line" on June 26–27; XXXIX Panzer Corps radioed "7th Panzer Division – Halt!," to which Rommel's old outfit irreverently replied, "Say again?," and kept plunging forward. By 1600hrs on the 28th, 12th Panzer Division entered Minsk; but the *Kessel* remained only half closed, since the willful Guderian headed east for Moscow rather than northeast toward Hoth and Minsk. Soviet units trickled out southeastward for another two days. To the west, while his infantry marched in the heat and dust on poor roads unwanted by the armor, Von Kluge dallied while methodically lining up his corps for the final assault on Minsk.

The advancing Guderian soon discovered what Korobkov had learned the hard way when earlier ordered to occupy and defend the "Stalin Line" – in many places it existed in name only. His 18th Panzer Division finally

SOVIET 6th RIFLE DIVISION TROOPS DEFEND BREST FORTRESS AGAINST GERMAN 45th INFANTRY DIVISION, JUNE 22–30, 1941 (pages 42–43)

The Russians built the Brest fortress between 1833 and 1842, at the confluence of the Bug and Mukhavets rivers; they improved the fortifications in 1878–88, and again in 1911–14. The fortress stood on four islands: central, northern, western and southern. The Treaty of Riga (1921) awarded Brest to the newly independent state of Poland, but the Red Army occupied it on September 22, 1939. (German troops under Guderian had captured it five days earlier, but had to hand it over to the Soviets.) The city and fortress stood in Guderian's way again in 1941, and would have to be reduced quickly.

The Soviet defenders belonged to elements of the 6th and 42nd Rifle Divisions, the 17th Frontier Guard Detachment, plus engineer, antitank, antiaircraft and other support units, totaling 7,000–8,000 men. The Austrian 45th Infantry Division provided most of the attackers, from I and III/IR 135 plus I and III/IR 130. Firing in support were 12 artillery batteries, 4th Nebelwerfer Regiment, 210mm howitzers, and two 600mm "Karl" siege guns firing rounds weighing over two tons.

German artillery fire began at 0305hrs on *Barbarossatag,* and pioneers crossed the Bug in asssault boats at 0319hrs, capturing bridges intact. By noon I/IR 135 had occupied much of the northern island and taken the city's rail station, while I/IR 130 took the southern island and five bridges over

the Bug and Mukhavets – thus bypassing most Soviet gun positions and opening the *Rollbahn* for Guderian's XXIV Panzer Corps. However, attempts to take the citadel by *coup de main* failed. By the 23rd most Soviet defenders had fallen back to the central island, destroying bridges behind them. Pockets of resistance held out under the command of majors and captains, and the front lines surged back and forth in seesaw fighting at the shortest ranges, while the ordnance of both sides destroyed the old brick fortifications around them.

In this scene, Soviet infantrymen, led by Lt Kizhevatov of the NKVD Frontier Guards (1), take up firing positions in a fort archway after overrunning an emplacement formerly occupied by a German MG34 crew (2); their weapons include a Maxim M1910 machine gun (3).

The combination of bunker-busting German heavy howitzers and mortars, flamethrowers, and the sheer exhaustion of relentless close-quarter fighting took their toll by June 29 and 30. The final blow fell on the 29th, when seven Junkers Ju 88 bombers of Kampfgeschwader 3 dropped two-ton bombs on the last pockets still holding out. Shell-shocked survivors, including wounded in the hospitals and the wives and children of Red Army officers, began to surrender. The garrison commander and the commissar committed suicide, but some 400 men went into captivity. By the end of June the Germans considered the battle officially over, although some defenders held out until the second half of July. Capturing Brest cost the 45th Infantry Division 414 dead.

closed the Minsk *Kessel* on the afternoon of June 29. The trap consisted of three main pockets, including those at Bialystok and Novogrudek. In places Red Army soldiers escaped through Guderian's weak southeastern cordon, while others fought to the last bullet or attacked in suicidal waves (especially at night), forcing many German units to form defensive Igels. Hunting down and capturing Soviets in dark forests, occupying rear areas and inventorying booty took until July 23.

By June 29, Stalin realized that Belorussia was lost; LtGen V.I. Kuznetsov's failure against Army Group North had contributed mightily to this disaster. The next day LtGen Yeremenko finally arrived at West Front headquarters with orders relieving Pavlov from command. Stalin made an example by executing the hapless Pavlov, so that all commanders "know defeatist behavior will be punished mercilessly." Yeremenko knew the terrain well, having led 6th Cavalry Corps into Poland in 1939 and to Kaunas in 1940, but he would hold command for only three days before becoming Marshal Timoshenko's deputy. On the other side of the lines, also on the 30th, Guderian flew to the Third Panzer Group command post to co-ordinate future operations (but also to conspire to defy Von Kluge by selective disobedience).

The Germans had long anticipated that capturing Minsk would mark a watershed; at that point Hitler and OKH were to decide if Von Bock's armor would turn north toward Leningrad, continue east, or execute some other course of action. With Rastenburg growing indecisive, Hoth and Guderian awaited instructions. Luftwaffe reconnaissance had earlier noticed that the road to Bobruisk was unprotected, and it was there that Guderian next directed his attention.

By early July both Panzer groups were approaching the River Berezina, whose defenders proved only a minor hindrance. Swampy headwaters in Hoth's area and along much of its east bank, and the numerous, long, wooden bridges, proved to be worse obstacles. It was here that Yeremenko vainly sought to make his first stand. Trying simultaneously to contain the Minsk pocket and stretch toward Smolensk robbed the Panzer groups of a coherent formation. This was especially true for Guderian's Second, aiming for Yelnia, which sprawled back over 150 miles. Hoth's Third meanwhile had to contend with terrible weather and terrain.

Once free to maneuver, 3rd Panzer Division made straight for Bobruisk. General Model escaped serious injury yet again, as the Soviets fought hard to hold the Bobruisk citadel and crossing site. Between June 30 and July 1 18th Panzer Division made a 60-mile raid to Borisov (originally Hoth's objective). 17th Panzer followed in support, both violating specific orders from Von Kluge, but securing yet another breach in the Soviet wall. (Von Kluge threatened both Hoth and Guderian with courts martial.) After a harrowing journey, the newly arrived 1st Moscow Motorized Division, with 1,000 tanks (including T-34s and KVs) and 500 guns, reached Borisov the next day and launched immediate counterattacks; these all failed.

Stavka tried to adjust to these new developments. Budenny's and Yeremenko's commands barely lasted a few days; Timoshenko took over leadership of the West and Reserve Fronts with Yeremenko as his deputy, and Stalin sent Budenny to Kiev. The Soviets had blundered through one crisis at Minsk and were about to face another, more severe one at Smolensk. For their part, the Germans reorganized their armored forces with effect from midnight July 2–3, when OKH created Fourth Panzer Army, formally subordinating Hoth and Guderian under Von Kluge while assigning the latter's infantry to Von Weichs and essentially creating the Second Army. Von Bock had de facto command of two separate armies, one fast and mechanized, the other slow and marching, and each with very different missions. While the tankers received much of the glory, German infantry did yeoman service as the massive shaft behind the Blitzkrieg's armored spearhead.

At Minsk the Germans claimed to have taken 341,000 POWs, and captured or destroyed 4,799 tanks, 9,427 guns and 1,777 aircraft. By inflicting these losses, plus an estimated similar number of wounded and missing, in about ten days, Army Group Center had arguably achieved its goals as set out in the numerous orders for *Barbarossa*. By July 2, Stavka realized that the "disorganized and much weakened forces of the first echelon of the Red Army cannot halt the advance of the enemy." However, German intelligence was already picking up indications of second- and

A Ju 87B Stuka pulls out of a dive after attacking a group of 80 Soviet tanks on August 1. Air–ground co-operation was essential for the success of Blitzkrieg, and Von Bock would miss Von Richthofen's VIII Fliegerkorps after August 3, when it was taken away from Army Group Center and shifted to the Leningrad Front. (NARA)

third-echelon forces occupying successive defensive lines on the road to Moscow. As Hitler wrote Mussolini on June 30, "The might and resources of the Red Army are far in excess of what we knew or even considered possible." Even so, few observers saw any end to *Barbarossa* other than an overwhelming German victory.

SMOLENSK

It should come as no surprise that it was Army Group Center that had scored the first major victory of *Barbarossa*. Its status as the campaign's *Schwerpunkt*, its two armored groups, two Fliegerkorps (including the elite VIII), plus Pavlov's extremely vulnerable position, made this practically inevitable. Von Leeb would never achieve a giant *Kessel* in the north, while down at Kiev Von Rundstedt would take another two months to double Von Bock's body count. With success at Minsk fresh in the Germans' minds, on June 30 OKH instructed Von Bock's headquarters to prepare to continue "operations in the direction of Smolensk."

A central feature of *Auftragstaktik* was that in the absence of explicit orders a subordinate would act in accordance with the higher commander's intent. It was within this framework that in early July – in violation of Hitler's instructions that the Minsk pockets be eliminated first, and largely on their own initiative – both Hoth and Guderian moved their Panzer groups toward Smolensk from positions north and south of Minsk. As the slower-marching infantry arrived at each of the smaller pockets they freed the armor to continue eastward. Every German leader knew that *Barbarossa*'s success depended upon not allowing the Red Army a moment's respite in which to re-establish a credible defense.

Guderian, and to a lesser extent Hoth, did not conceal their belief that Moscow should be the *Ostheer*'s main goal. In his June 22 order of the day the former went so far as to say, "The objective is Moscow – every man must know this!" This opinion agreed with neither the various *Barbarossa* directives, nor Hitler's oft-stated belief that Moscow "is not very important." However, neither Stalin, Timoshenko nor Zhukov had any knowledge of this – another failure of the otherwise very effective Soviet spy network. For the remainder of the summer the Soviets threw every possible obstacle in Von Bock's way, to the detriment of their defenses along other fronts.

Preliminaries

At Minsk, Von Bock had supposedly crushed everything the Soviets had with which to defend Moscow. Thus the exposed tips of both Panzer spearheads received a nasty surprise when, on July 4, Stavka ordered Timoshenko to "organize a reliable defense, concentrate reserves... deliver counterstrokes along the Lepel, Borisov and Bobruisk axes." 20th Army plus 5th and 7th Mechanized Corps guarded the middle Berezina due west of the "River Gate." Lieutenant-General P.A. Kurochkin's 128th, 153rd, 229th, 233rd, 73rd, 18th & 137th Rifle Divisions blunted the drive of Guderian's northernmost XLVII Panzer Corps. Guderian's central corps, XLVI Panzer, had it easier; and his southern thrust by XXIV Panzer Corps had it easiest of all near Rogatchev, despite the opposition of 36 artillery batteries and the 117th Rifle Division on the east bank.

Many Soviet reinforcements from all across the USSR arrived on trains and often went directly to the fighting, occasionally very close by. The quality of their training and leadership was uneven, but these reinforcements were essential for plugging holes in the Soviet lines. (From the fonds of the RGAKFD at Krasnogorsk)

Field Marshal Günther Von Kluge (center) was a solid if unspectacular performer, but troublesome as both a superior and a subordinate. He earned his well-deserved reputation for deliberate and old-fashioned (i.e., non-Blitzkrieg) leadership in France and the USSR, to the frustration of more decisive commanders. He still managed to get into the thick of battle, however, and like the more venturesome Guderian he was sometimes forced to draw his personal weapon for self defense. (USAMHI)

Meanwhile, Hoth was dangerously spread out, with a 100-mile gap between his XXXIX Panzer Corps near Vitebsk and LVII Panzer Corps at Polotsk and Disna. Following orders to "destroy the Lepel enemy concentration," the Soviet 5th and 7th Mechanized Corps now turned their attention on XXXIX Panzer Corps, just slightly north of Guderian's XLVII Panzer; if executed properly, the Red Army attack would split the seam between the two Panzer groups. This meeting engagement, centered on Senno, initially pushed 7th Panzer Division back 20 miles, and eventually involved 12th, 17th and 18th Panzer as well. Of the 2,000 mostly obsolete tanks available to the two Soviet mechanized corps, only 70 percent even made it to the battlefield, and after five days the Germans had destroyed 832 of these. Beaten, the remnants of 5th and 7th Mechanized withdrew toward Smolensk.

In order to give Timoshenko no opportunity to establish his second echelon, XXXIX Panzer Corps took up the pursuit. Its 7th Panzer Division, followed by 20th, lay strung out along the one usable road from Lepel to Vitebsk; rain slowed their advance and bought the Soviets time; with their 22nd Army holding a 175-mile front with six weak divisions, they needed such a pause. Elsewhere, Hoth's men had to cross 100 wooden bridges on the 50-mile long road from Borisov to Lepel — all of which collapsed under the weight of a modern army. Stavka noticed the vulnerable flanks of the Panzer groups from the start, but lacked the means to defeat them. Soon the bulk of Timoshenko's defenders were streaming east; with the Berezina line abandoned, the next stop was the Dvina and Dnepr rivers.

Toward Smolensk

Stalin had sent the Reserve Front forward on July 1, too soon and not massed – creating a counteroffensive in name only. Fortunately for the Russians, the Germans had significant troubles of their own. Strategically, since *Barbarossa*'s inception, Minsk marked the point when Hitler would decide what to do during the second phase of the campaign. With forces

When Hoth's troops arrived at Ulla they discovered the bridge over the western Dvina destroyed (left); engineers constructed the new bridge to the right. (USAMHI)

in place and ready to continue the advance, he nevertheless deferred that decision. German strategic intelligence continued to flounder. At a July 8 conference at Rastenburg they put Timoshenko's strength at 11 divisions; in reality Army Group Center faced 66 (24 in first echelon, 37 actually in position). Three days later Halder wrote that the Soviets had no reserves behind the fighting front; in fact, Stavka had created reserves that OKW could only envy.

The Germans' final problem was Von Kluge, who now suffered a crisis of confidence in his new role as a Panzer Army commander. On July 5 he complained to OKW that he could not control Hoth and Guderian. Von Brauchitsch reminded him that his duty was not to micromanage his Panzer commanders, and advised him to give these capable subordinates free rein, creating his *Schwerpunkt* with the one who first gained freedom of action. A day later a frustrated Von Bock admonished Von Kluge to "Make a [Panzer] fist – somewhere." An esssential prerequisite for creating a pocket at Smolensk was for Hoth and Guderian to rupture the Dvina–Dnepr line at Vitebsk and Mogilev.

Hoth continued towards Vitebsk and Polotsk, thunderstorms and rising rivers hampering his every step. Five or six new Red Army divisions established defensive positions at Polotsk astride both banks of the Dvina. After racing 120 miles in 24 hours, 19th Panzer Division seized a bridge intact at Disna on July 4, and 18th and 14th Motorized Divisions provided flank protection while engineers built a second bridge. On the same day 7th Panzer Division ran into Konev's 19th Army defenses at Vitebsk, and halted to wait for Strauss's infantry.

At Disna, Red Army counterattacks were supported by aircraft and artillery. On July 5, heavily armored *Sturmoviki* attacked 7th Panzer without suffering a loss, despite some planes taking 200 hits. Pressure at Disna came from an unexpected source: 27th Army, being shoved southeastward by Army Group North. Nevertheless, Hoth's vanguards continued to expand their bridgeheads. With 7th Panzer stalled before Vitebsk, Hoth opted for the indirect approach. Between July 5 and 7, 20th Panzer Division and

7TH PANZER AND 29TH MOTORIZED INFANTRY DIVISIONS LINK UP, CLOSING THE SMOLENSK *KESSEL*, JULY 16 1941
(pages 50–51)

Smolensk sits at a crossroads of western Russia, on the main route of advance from central Europe toward Moscow. Over the centuries it has long been a commercial, religious and administrative center, and often the objective of military operations.

The 7th Panzer Division (which had been commanded by Erwin Rommel during the western campaign of May–June 1940) led Hoth's Third Panzer Group during the first three weeks of *Barbarossa*. Sweeping clockwise from Vitebsk toward Smolensk from the north, it was about to close Von Bock's second major encirclement of the campaign. On the evening of July 15 elements of the division reached the Smolensk–Moscow highway near Yartsevo; the four-lane road was packed with Soviet traffic, the great majority of it still heading toward the west, and doom. Some way farther on was the major railway line, also busy with trains heading westwards. The 7th Panzer Division's gunners wreaked havoc among the road convoys and rail traffic.

Meanwhile, the 29th Motorized Infantry Division had so far been following in the wake of Guderian's Second Panzer Group. After closing one of the numerous encirclements that made up the Minsk *Kessel*, the "Falcon" Division raced northeastward toward Smolensk, and in heavy fighting finally succeeded in establishing a bridgehead across the Dnepr at Kopys by July 11. They needed support from Sturmgeschütz Abteilung 203, a heavy Flak battery, an antitank battalion and corps engineers to secure their foothold, and Soviet counter-attacks were so heavy that their dead were piled in heaps. On the 16th the division – described by Guderian as "a splendid unit" – entered Smolensk from the southwest; by that evening it had traversed the southern half of the city and was crossing the Dnepr onto the much more stoutly defended northern bank. Fighting in the city streets caused heavy casualties on both sides, and lasted until July 22. While the bulk of the 29th Division was thus engaged, however, its reconnaissance elements pushed on eastward, and linked up with troops of the 7th Panzer. This scene reconstructs such a meeting.

On the rail embankment in the background, under skies haunted by the Stukas of Von Richthofen's Fliegerkorps VIII, flatcars are still loaded with new T-34 tanks destined for the front. Crewmen from a PzKw 38(t) (1) of the 7th Panzer Division's reinforced Panzer Regiment 25 stretch their legs while awaiting orders; the tank bears the division's yellow runic symbol, and the white temporary marking of Third Panzer Group – a stylized "Hh" for Hoth. It was significant that the *Ostheer* still had to employ more than 600 of these Czech tanks – note the extra-large tactical recognition numbers painted on the turret. Farther off is an SdKfz 232(Fu) radio-equipped armored car (2) of 29th Motorized Infantry's divisional Aufklärungs Abteilung, marked with the white "G" of Guderian's Second Panzer Group. A group of senior officers (3) speculate about the next objective – assumed at this stage by many German soldiers, from Army Chief of Staff Franz Halder down to the lowliest *Landser*, to be Moscow. Meanwhile infantrymen (4) deploy to provide local security, and guard a few of the 300,000-plus Soviet prisoners (5) who were rounded up in the Smolensk *Kessel*.

A heavily laden group of infantry occupy the burning village of Lutky, near Vitebsk, on July 15. The spare barrels, ammunition boxes and sustained-fire tripod for the MG34 squad machine gun are recognizable among their burdens. (USAMHI)

20th Motorized encountered 62nd Rifle Corps defenses upriver at Ulla. With support from Von Richthofen's "flying artillery" they sent across two waves of assault boats, and finally overcame the numerous bunkers late on July 8; 20th Panzer's Kampfgruppe "Von Bismarck" assaulted Vitebsk from the rear the next morning. Red Army units counterattacked desperately against the bridgeheads and the smoldering city in an attempt to throw them back, but ultimately Hoth's men made a deadly crack in Timoshenko's Dvina–Dnepr line.

About ten weak divisions of Erashkov's 22nd Army plus some 27th Army stragglers sat astride the boundary between Army Groups North and Center near Nevel. Against Von Bock's wishes, higher headquarters ordered his LVII Panzer Corps to liquidate this force. Spread too thin to close the trap at Nevel, this diversion accomplished very little. Amid confusion, 19th Panzer Division continued to Velikie Luki and captured the town on the 20th, only to give it back to the Red Army when the division was redirected yet again; the same troops would have to retake it at a higher cost a month later. This Nevel detour reduced Hoth to only one armored corps on his main axis, severely curtailing his ability to influence events at this critical time.

Also on July 4, Guderian's 4th Panzer Division reached Bychov on the Dnepr, a well-defended town complete with a broad antitank ditch. They managed to cross the river, only to have the Soviets chase them back to the west bank and demolish the bridge. To the north, Model's 3rd Panzer Division crossed the Dnepr at Rogatchev aided by its wading tanks – despite the fact that the 800-yard-wide river was in flood. By 0445hrs on July 5, 4th Panzer Division engineers had thrown a new bridge across and continued the assault with the support of 210mm howitzers; the bridge collapsed at 0730hrs, but would be rebuilt by 1100hrs.

For Second Panzer Group, the Stalin Line did not appear to be a hollow shell. The operational rate for tanks of 3rd and 18th Panzer Divisions stood at only 35 percent and 58 percent. With the German rail and logistics system severely disrupted at Brest, 4th Panzer Division sent a staff major all the way to Germany to scrounge for spare parts. On July 11, 87th Infantry Division received its first reinforcements since June 22 – 350 men, which they promptly had to hand over to Guderian. Initially repulsed on the left, Guderian shifted his *Schwerpunkt* first to the right and then to his center. The fight along the Dnepr raged during July 7–16, and as the Soviets retreated they managed to destroy many bridges. Guderian's new attack axis would send him straight for the fortress town of Mogilev.

Despite supply difficulties and stiff resistance, the Germans had turned the Dvina–Dnepr line into a shambles. From his bridgehead at Ulla, Hoth wrecked Timoshenko's right, separating 27th, 22nd and 20th Armies so they could be defeated in detail. Three infantry corps of the Ninth Army soon arrived at Vitebsk, freeing Hoth's armor to continue advancing. Strauss now dealt directly with Konev's 19th Army, and air reconnaissance detected a general Soviet exodus toward Smolensk.

Guderian's success on the Dnepr had been less spectacular than Hoth's. Despite rougher terrain and poorer roads in its sector, the Third Panzer Group enjoyed a much straighter route to Moscow, placing Hoth in a better strategic position. Therefore Von Bock recommended to Von Kluge that Fourth Panzer Army immediately reinforce Hoth, making him the *Schwerpunkt* of Army Group Center. Von Kluge hesitated; but on this occasion events bore him out. On July 10 and 11, Second Panzer Group's attack with 450 operational tanks achieved bridgeheads over the Dnepr at Shklov (XLVI Panzer Corps) and Kopys (XLVII Panzer Corps), and for a second time at Bychov (XXIV Panzer Corps). By the 14th, Von Bock ordered the Fourth Panzer Army to continue its advance to the line Belyy–Yartsevo–Yelnia.

On Guderian's right, Mogilev was encircled on July 17 where units of 61st Rifle and 20th Mechanized Corps established a fortress-like defense of the city. These forces under MajGen M.T. Romanov – especially 172nd Rifle Division – held out until July 27 with the help of air-dropped supplies. The defenders' efforts against 23rd, 15th, 7th and 78th Infantry Divisions earned the accolades "Gallant Mogilev" and "Russian Madrid." (The Spanish Civil War was still a fresh memory.) Eventually more than 35,000 *frontoviki* marched into captivity; Romanov escaped the trap, only to be captured by the Germans later and executed as a partisan. XXIV Panzer Corps crossed the Dnepr south of the town, and made for Krichev.

The forward obvserver for a light field howitzer battery – perched atop a haystack, with "scissors" binoculars – searches for targets, while his radio operator below relays instructions. Quick communications and accurate fire adjustment somewhat compensated for the relatively smaller German artillery branch. (USAMHI)

A tank unit with mixed Czech and German vehicles – thus probably from 6th, 7th or 12th Panzer Division – is towing its own fuel trailers as it drives through a Russian city. German logistics often failed even with such a basic requirement as getting fuel forward to keep the Panzers rolling; Hoth was halted by such a shortage on October 4 during the Viazma/Bryansk battles. (HITM)

Meanwhile the foot-slogging German infantry struggled to keep up with their armor, reduce the encircled pockets, and fight off partisan attacks that were growing in boldness and intensity. The 35th Infantry Division spent the first three months of *Barbarossa* marching 500 miles, or an average of 20 miles per day. Men from 137th Infantry Division tore Russian houses apart and used the planks to cross swamps. Whatever rest-days the infantry enjoyed were often more for the benefit of their thousands of draft horses than for the *Landsers*.

Hitler continued to fret over the ability of Army Groups North and South to accomplish their missions without drawing on Von Bock's armor for reinforcements. On July 13 the Germans captured documents ordering Timoshenko to hold the Dvina–Dnepr line and counterattack. The previous day Stavka (via Zhukov) had instructed him to "Immediately organize a powerful and co-ordinated counterstroke by all available forces from Smolensk, Orsha, Polotsk and Nevel regions to liquidate the enemy penetration [Hoth] at Vitebsk... [and to] conduct active operations along the Gomel and Bobruisk axes to exert pressure on the rear of the enemy's Bobruisk grouping [Guderian]." This was good news for Hitler and Halder, since it indicated that the Soviets had no intention of withdrawing into the interior – the dreaded 1812 gambit. However, it was their first inkling of what Guderian would later call the "Timoshenko Offensive", and hinted at threats to Von Bock's southern flank. By July 5, Hitler had already been pondering the second phase of the invasion for a week. A few days later OKH began toying with the idea of sending Guderian to Army Group South and Kiev. Stavka's instructions to Timoshenko now served to support this option.

Closing the trap

Now across the Dvina–Dnepr line, Army Group Center set itself to close the Smolensk *Kessel* and continue eastward. After the war Yeremenko wrote that "There were no troops... to prevent the enemy from crossing the Dnepr and then advancing in any direction he pleased." Von Bock's *Schwerpunkt* now clearly lay on his southern flank: Guderian had three times as much armor as Hoth, while Second Army fielded the unusually high number of seven corps (VII, IX, XII, XIII, LXVIII, LIII and XXXV).

One reason that the Sturmgeschütz was so important to the Germans: their mainly horse-drawn artillery often lagged far to the rear of the fighting, making displacing to new positions a slow process. The standard German infantry division still included some 6,000 horses, for its artillery, supply train, and part of its reconnaissance element. (HITM)

On July 11, XLVI Panzer Corps broke out of the Shklov bridgehead and made for Yelnia; XLVII Panzer Corps went from Kopys toward Orsha, while XXIV Panzer Corps covered Guderian's right. A day later his men split 13th and 20th Armies, outflanking Orsha and advancing almost to Mogilev. Air activity was intense: II Fliegerkorps flew 885 sorties on July 14 against 21st Army, and 615 sorties two days later. Such responses as the Soviets could muster were ineffectual. The 13th Army's new commander, Remizov, was wounded, and replaced by LtGen V.F. Gerasimenko. Just to show that he was not ignoring Smolensk, Guderian sent 29th Motorized Division in that direction. Now finally clear of Vitebsk, Hoth's 7th Panzer Division closed in on Smolensk from the north, and by July 13 only 25 miles separated it from Guderian's 29th Motorized. Two days later the 7th "Rommeled" into Yartsevo, cutting the main road and rail line into Smolensk and sealing the fate of the city and most of its defenders. However, as mentioned above, both Hoth and Strauss had been stripped of valuable assets, and were ordered to maintain contact with Army Group North in addition to continuing their push east; many of their units were too far north to help close the pocket.

General Wolfram von Richthofen (right) and his VIII Fliegerkorps set the standard for close air support by any air force during World War II; he had been specializing in such operations since the Spanish Civil War. A hands-on leader comfortable near the fighting, Von Richthofen often landed in his Fieseler Storch liaison aircraft to confer directly with the army commanders he was supporting. (Podzun)

Soviet T-26 tanks move out as dug-in infantry look on. Not considered to be the USSR's likely main defensive effort, the West Front had to make do with second-rate equipment and weaker numbers – a fact that spelled doom for many of Pavlov's counterattacks. Later in the campaign the T-26 was often still the only tank type available. (Elukka)

By the evening of July 15 the 29th Motorized Division arrived at the southwest end of the city – a ghost town which paid mute tribute to Stalin's scorched-earth policy. The old part, south of the Dnepr, was occupied by Guderian's men within 24 hours. The Soviet defenders launched repeated counterattacks, especially when the Germans tried to cross over to the north bank, and 29th Motorized had to fight these off until July 22.

Inside the *Kessel*

Before the trap closed, trains with reinforcements were pulling out of Bryansk for Smolensk every ten minutes. Many of these forces manned the farther reaches of the pocket; the defense of the city itself left much to be desired. What had been intended to be a bastion was in fact a feeble crust, held by a couple of Gen Lukin's weak divisions plus militia battalions, totaling 18,000 men; many of the 16th Army units had been bled off to fight Hoth near Demidov. Stalin nevertheless enforced "stand until the last man" orders upon Stavka and local commanders. Demolition of the city's bridges slowed the German advance and allowed 129th Rifle Division to augment the defense of the north bank. Tactically, Red Army units acquitted themselves well, especially in house-to-house fighting, and fighting around Smolensk dragged on for nearly five days. Inside the pocket the NKVD rounded up nearly 104,000 Red Army stragglers and returned them to the fighting. Although the Germans held the city proper in the face of Soviet counterattacks, they never completely sealed off the pocket.

Air fighting was intense as the Luftwaffe interdicted rail lines leading into the city. Between July 10 and the end of the month the Germans launched 12,653 sorties and the Soviets approximately 5,200. When VIII Fliegerkorps departed north on August 3 for the hoped-for climactic battle of Leningrad the Soviet air effort increased dramatically. Luftwaffe strength was further dissipated by bombing raids on Moscow beginning on the night of July 21. These were mainly symbolic, and they had little material effect; in over three-quarters of the 76 raids conducted over the next month, fewer than ten bombers participated. All told, the raids killed only 736 Muscovites and wounded 3,513 more.

The Germans considered the Smolensk trap officially closed on July 26, but Von Bock had already complained in his diary that "it has a hole" – the ten-mile gap near Yartsevo and Solovevo through which, between

July 31 and August 4, substantial portions of 16th and 20th Armies escaped the *Kessel*. Von Bock ordered Hoth and Strauss to continue farther south to compensate for Guderian's eastward movement. The 7th Panzer Division again bore the brunt of the fighting, fending off Rokossovsky's infantry attacks, which came supported by 80 to 100 tanks. Of the division's 284 Panzers, only 118 were operational; of its 166 damaged tanks, 70 were beyond repair. A rumored German airborne operation near Yartsevo was little more than aerial resupply of the hard-pressed 7th Panzer.

On August 5, Von Bock announced the conclusion of the battle of Smolensk and the capture of 302,000 POWs, 3,205 tanks, 3,120 guns and 1,098 aircraft. The previous day Hitler had flown to Army Group Center headquarters to offer his congratulations in person. The Führer reaffirmed his decision to divert Second and Third Panzer Groups towards Kiev and Leningrad respectively; but he also authorized limited offensives from the vicinity of Yelnia. Von Bock, Hoth and Guderian all approved, since they believed that the Soviets had only the barest means left for a defense of Moscow. They had no way of knowing that only five days earlier Stalin had ordered Zhukov to eliminate the threat to his capital represented by the Yelnia salient. At the August 4 meeting Hitler ordered Yelnia be held at all costs, devoting ten divisions to the effort. With Von Richthofen transferred to Leningrad, only portions of II Fliegerkorps remained to provide close air support. Defending the salient, advancing on Moscow, and assisting its two neighboring army groups would have been a tough enough mission for Von Bock, even if OKH had had a clear idea of where *Barbarossa* was going next.

ADJUSTMENTS

It is unsurprising that in a campaign as vast and complex as *Barbarossa*, the combatants had to make numerous alterations to their plans, organization, operations and in many other areas. For reasons of thematic continuity, this chapter will discuss various modifications undertaken by both sides during and immediately after the battle for Smolensk.

Although the unrealistic prewar plans to launch an immediate counteroffensive into Germany were quickly forgotten, the Soviet desire to counterattack – somewhere – remained. After the failure of their Grodno attacks Stalin urged Timoshenko to take decisive action; and various echelons of command and other control relationships were eliminated as inefficient wastes of precious manpower.

On the other side of the lines, the Germans moved quickly from a mood of celebration to the hard work of deciding what to do next. After Smolensk neither Hitler, OKW, OKH, nor commanders in the field could agree on the logical next move. From before mid-July to beyond mid-August a colossal power struggle hamstrung the Wehrmacht senior leadership, until the Führer imposed his will on the generals in late August. By mid-summer Von Bock's men, in exposed salients and at the end of their logistical umbilical cords, were suffering badly under the flurry of Soviet counterpunching. Meanwhile, major developments occurred to the north and south, while both armies prepared for the ultimate battle for Moscow.

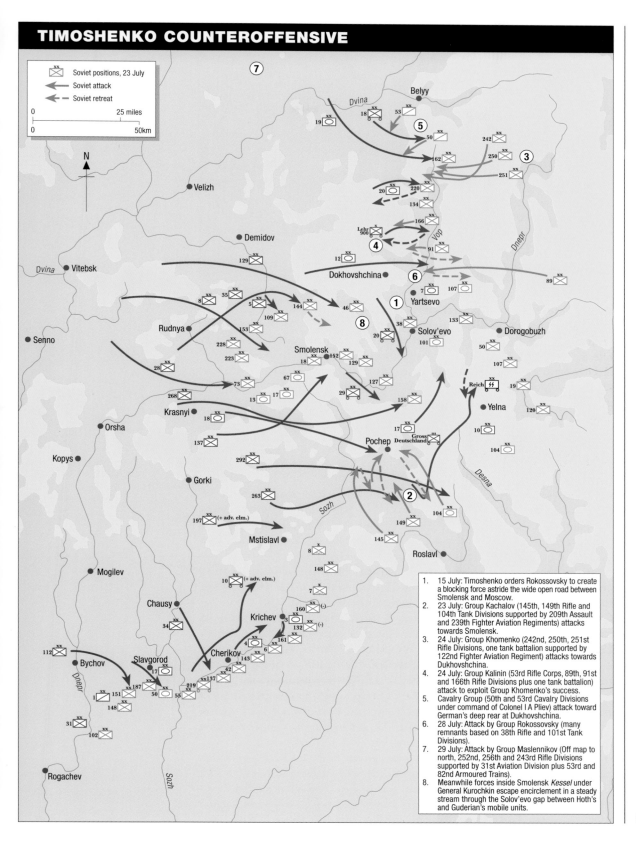

Soviet positions, 23 July

Soviet attack

Soviet retreat

0   25 miles

0   50km

N

Map labels: Belyy, Dvina, Velizh, Demidov, Dvina, Vitebsk, Dokhovshchina, Yartsevo, Solov'evo, Dorogobuzh, Rudnya, Smolensk, Senno, Krasnyi, Orsha, Yelna, Pochep, Gross Deutschland, Reich, Kopys, Gorki, Sozh, Mstislavl, Roslavl, Mogilev, Chausy, Krichev, Cherikov, Bychov, Slavgorod, Dnepr, Desna, Rogachev, Sozh

1. 15 July: Timoshenko orders Rokossovsky to create a blocking force astride the wide open road between Smolensk and Moscow.
2. 23 July: Group Kachalov (145th, 149th Rifle and 104th Tank Divisions supported by 209th Assault and 239th Fighter Aviation Regiments) attacks towards Smolensk.
3. 24 July: Group Khomenko (242nd, 250th, 251st Rifle Divisions, one tank battalion supported by 122nd Fighter Aviation Regiment) attacks towards Dukhovshchina.
4. 24 July: Group Kalinin (53rd Rifle Corps, 89th, 91st and 166th Rifle Divisions plus one tank battalion) attack to exploit Group Khomenko's success.
5. Cavalry Group (50th and 53rd Cavalry Divisions under command of Colonel I A Pliev) attack toward German's deep rear at Dukhovshchina.
6. 28 July: Attack by Group Rokossovsky (many remnants based on 38th Rifle and 101st Tank Divisions).
7. 29 July: Attack by Group Maslennikov (Off map to north, 252nd, 256th and 243rd Rifle Divisions supported by 31st Aviation Division plus 53rd and 82nd Armoured Trains).
8. Meanwhile forces inside Smolensk *Kessel* under General Kurochkin escape encirclement in a steady stream through the Solov'evo gap between Hoth's and Guderian's mobile units.

The Timoshenko counteroffensive

While the jaws of Von Bock's Panzer groups closed on the Smolensk pocket, Stavka struggled to regain the initiative. The Germans already had a copy of the July 13 order instructing Timoshenko to attack. Three days later the marshal complained to Moscow that he had "insufficient strength to cover Yartsevo, Viazma and Moscow. The main thing is no tanks." Stavka (through Zhukov) reiterated its orders on the 20th, essentially telling the West Front to use four armies to encircle the Germans then attempting to surround Smolensk, and save the 16th, 19th and 20th Armies. The same order demanded "operations by larger groups" than Timoshenko's previous attacks by two or three divisions. Stavka instructed him to create five attack groups, each loosely based on a field army and named after its commander: 29th Army (LtGen I.I. Maslinnikov), 30th Army (MajGen V.A. Khomenko), 24th Army (MajGen S.A. Kalinin), 28th Army (LtGen V.I. Kachalov) – all four NKVD generals; plus an ad hoc group under MajGen K.K. Rokossovsky. Initially these forces were all supposed to attack on July 21.

Group Kachalov moved out first, on the 23rd; it was soon creating problems for Guderian, and by July 27 it looked as if the 10th Panzer Division and "Grossdeutschland" might become cut off. Guderian responded with a counterattack towards the important communications node at Roslavl. By July 31, XXIV Panzer Corps (3rd & 4th Panzer Divisions) and VII Army Corps (197th, 23rd & 78th Infantry Divisions) were attacking eastward from Krichev into Kachalov's rear; a day later IX Army Corps (263rd & 292nd Infantry Divisions) assaulted southward, sealing Group Kachalov's fate. The fight against this apparently most serious of the threats to Army Group Center was over by August 7. (Even though Gen Kachalov had died in battle in a Soviet tank, Commissar Lev Mekhlis had him branded as a traitor.)

Groups Kalinin and Khomenko attacked on July 24. VIII Fliegerkorps had not yet departed for Army Group North, so Bf 109s mauled the Soviet close support effort. Kalinin's mission was to exploit Kachalov's "success;" consequently neither attack achieved much, and both were soon turned back. The same day ColGen O.I. Gorodovikov's Cavalry Group (32nd, 43rd

& 47th Cavalry Divisions supported by 232nd Rifle Division) began causing trouble across Guderian's and Von Weich's lines of communication southwest of Bobruisk. Group Maslinnikov (off the map to the north) attacked on July 29, but also achieved little.

Arguably the weakest group had the greatest impact. Rokossovsky had the mission of halting the German direct advance on Viazma and Moscow, but started with a force of only two rifle and four artillery regiments. He soon collected stragglers of 38th Rifle Division plus about 90 tanks. His assault first blunted, then actually drove back the advance of 7th Panzer and 20th Motorized Divisions. Von Bock added 17th Panzer, yet still could neither displace Rokossovsky's men, nor close the Solovevo gap through the ring around Smolensk.

Kachalov's attacks, Rokossovsky's stubbornness, the fact that Von Kluge was temporarily out of contact, and other factors all combined to cause the Germans momentary consternation. But Von Bock had foreknowledge of the Timoshenko offensive, had dispatched the Luftwaffe to attack Soviet assembly areas, and had generally halted the unco-ordinated and piecemeal operations. When the Smolensk *Kessel* slammed shut on about July 27–28, Stavka changed Timoshenko's mission from relieving the trapped defenders to escaping encirclement. In the marshal's after-action report to Stalin he wrote that he "gave all the reinforcements that I could to Khomenko and Kalinin. But you know I had no guns, no aircraft and very few personnel."

The German crisis of command

Hitler was deathly superstitious about following Napoleon's footsteps to Moscow. As early as the end of June he was considering a second phase for *Barbarossa*, but was clear that it did not include Moscow. The plan since the previous December had been to send Hoth and Guderian north and south after Smolensk. In diary entries of June 30 and July 8, Halder agreed with this thinking; infantry would be enough to take Moscow. However, there was no unanimity among the German leadership.

Hitler resorted to issuing Führer directives – his first (No.33) on July 19, without even consulting his staff. Succinctly, the directive stated that Von Bock would advance on Moscow with infantry only. By this time Halder had changed his mind and tried to persuade Hitler to continue committing the armor to this axis. His arguments backfired when he told Hitler that owing to logistics problems Second and Ninth Armies could not advance on Moscow until August 10; the Führer replied that in that case he would send the tanks north and south as planned.

By the second half of July, German euphoria had cooled; but in view of the vast territory taken, estimated Soviet casualties of 3 million dead and wounded, and another million captured, it was incomprehensible to Hitler that the enemy could sustain a credible defense. He departed on a tour of army group headquarters to speak directly to field commanders, especially those of the Panzer groups.

On July 23 he issued a supplement to his earlier directive. (*Ergänzung* can also be translated as "completion.") He issued Directive No.34 on July 30 (this was at least written with Jodl's help), followed by another Supplement on August 12. (See Campaign 148 for a full description.) At each step the command structure had to retool its thinking. On August 7 two key figures, Jodl at OKW and Halder at OKH, met to discuss Moscow for the "first time that anyone can remember." (Gen Warlimont) Three days later both headquarters issued a joint situation report recommending the Moscow option. On the 18th, OKH submitted a *Denkschrift* (Study), supposedly for Von Brauchitsch's eyes only, claiming that the *Ostheer* only had enough resources and, most importantly, time for one objective in what was left of 1941: Moscow. However, the Wehrmacht leadership could not present a united front to dissuade the Führer from the southern option. At one point Guderian told Von Bock and Halder that he could not turn south away from Moscow because of his troops' exhaustion – yet just one day later, when confronted by Hitler, he said that he could do exactly that (to Halder's fury).

Throughout most of this critical period Soviet reactions had a decisive effect on German thinking. The inability of Army Groups North and South to encircle and eliminate large numbers of Red Army troops had left Von Bock's flanks vulnerable. (Von Leeb and Von Rundstedt each had only one Panzer group, so double envelopments were difficult, if not impossible.) Soviet moves on the flanks made German plans obsolete before they could be executed, and shook Hitler's confidence – he no longer "walked with the assurance of a sleepwalker."

Hitler broke the intellectual logjam on August 21 with his own *Denkschrift*. He stated that sending the Panzer groups north and south and not toward Moscow was:

> *not a new proposition, but a fact that I have clearly and unequivocally stated since the beginning of the operation... The principal object that must yet be achieved before the onset of winter is not the capture of Moscow, but rather, in the south the occupation of the Crimea and the industrial and coal region of the Donets.*

The document went on to accuse Von Brauchitsch of caving in to the army group commanders. Ultimately, Hitler authorized both the Kiev and Moscow options, but at least he had resolved the matter of sequencing: he would first destroy Red Army forces in the field.

Yelnia

XLVI Panzer Corps seized the Yelnia bridgehead over the Desna river on July 20. It was seen as a temporary halt; most commanders assumed that they would resume the advance on Moscow as soon as the infantry had tidied up the Smolensk and neighboring pockets, and Yelnia would serve as the ideal jumping-off point for the year's last big push. However, the second half of July coincided with the crisis of command at Rastenburg; German units at Yelnia had only had an early taste of what would turn out to be a ten-week defensive struggle – and in view of its "temporary" nature, the salient had been chosen neither for its defensive qualities nor for its suitability for reinforcement and resupply.

While defensive doctrine did not receive the same emphasis as offensive in the German Army, it was not neglected; but the Poles and western allies had never severely tested German defenses. Less than two months into the campaign, and with the mass of Von Bock's armor fighting to the north and south, Zhukov now sought to make Yelnia a lightning rod for a series of deadly assaults. The end result was Germany's first operational

withdrawal in World War II.

A destroyed Soviet BM-13 Katyusha rocket launcher. NKVD troops were the only ones permitted to fire this secret weapon upon its introduction in July 1941. (Nik Cornish at Stavka)

Elements of 10th Panzer Division and SS "Reich" initially occupied Yelnia. It took Timoshenko only three days to assemble his attack forces, and they began hitting the German positions for the next two weeks. Their operational mission was to relieve their trapped comrades inside the Smolensk encirclement by September 8. Guderian's men often had to fend off a dozen attacks per day, while ammunition and reserves ran dangerously low. Close proximity to Smolensk became a German asset as that *Kessel* was reduced, freeing up infantry and the Luftwaffe's I Flak Corps for duty at Yelnia.

With Lukin's surrender at Smolensk the immediate need for the Soviets to carry the attack forward so vigorously diminished. By the middle of August most of Von Bock's tanks began to depart in the directions of Leningrad and Kiev, so the Fourth and Ninth Armies took over the sector's defense. The bulk of Kesselring's two Fliegerkorps also flew north and south. Simultaneously, while the Germans had advanced beyond the reach of their logistical tether, the Soviets retreated back along their lines of supply. As Army Group Center abdicated the battlefield initiative, Timoshenko seized it. By August 11 the Soviets were assaulting all along Von Bock's front. Timoshenko's subordinate 19th Army (reinforced by 101st Tank Division and 43rd Mixed Aviation Division) achieved a six-mile penetration across the River Vop. As Timoshenko pounded German positions north of the salient, Zhukov, now commanding the Reserve Front, lavished his attention on Yelnia. His main assett would be MajGen K.I.Rakutin's 24th Army; simultaneously, MajGen L.M. Dovator led the 50th and 53rd Cavalry Divisions on a raid deep into the German rear.

To the German soldier on the ground there seemed to be no shortage of Soviet infantry, ordnance or close air support. Assaults in battalion strength, parachute drops behind their lines and night attacks became common. Here the unsuitability of the terrain surrounding the German positions became fatal for many a *Landser*: the wounded had to wait until dark for medical evacuation away from their exposed locations. They could not even count on help in the form of counterattacks by armor and motorized troops, since Guderian's mobile forces were fighting back the Bryansk Front attacks, reducing the Roslavl threat, and making preparations for the upcoming operation against Kiev.

The beginning of the end of the Yelnia salient came on August 30 when, following a three-hour artillery preparation, the Soviets stove in 23rd Infantry Division to a depth of six miles. On September 2, Von Brauchitsch, Halder and Von Bock all agreed to abandon Yelnia, and the order went out the next evening. IX and XX Army Corps executed a withdrawal on the 5th, and the Soviet 100th, 103rd, 309th and 120th Rifle Divisions reoccupied the town from the following day.

The drive south

The *Ostheer* was reorganized again on July 27, when Von Kluge was removed from command of Fourth Panzer Army; Von Bock and his two Panzer group leaders felt a sense of relief, but Hoth's joy was short-lived: he had lost most of his armor to Army Group North and, as of August 5, he also commanded the Ninth Army in place of the ailing Strauss. Guderian, however, raced on with his newly minted Armeegruppe Guderian, and did not allow details such as reducing the Smolensk pocket or fighting a defensive battle at Yelnia to stop him.

When attempts to capture the tactically desirable bridges at Orsha, Mogilev and Rogatchev failed, Guderian crossed the Dnepr elsewhere, making those towns irrelevant. In typical Blitzkrieg fashion he left Mogilev to the Ninth Army infantry, believing that the Soviets there were too weak and disorganized to present a threat. He ordered IX Army Corps to continue toward Roslavl all night on August 2–3, and marched at the head of the column to ensure his orders were carried out. On the 3rd, IX Corps linked up with Von Schweppenburg's XXIV Panzer Corps, thereby encircling more than 38,000 defenders and capturing 250 tanks and 713 guns.

At Krichev, on August 14, 16,000 POWs of the resuscitated 13th Army were taken by XXIV Panzer plus VII and XIII Army Corps troops. Von Weichs had the mission of taking Gomel, but by August 12 had not yet attacked owing to mud and shortage of ammunition. By the time the

Destined to play critical roles in the defense along the Moscow axis, Generals Zhukov (second from left) and Yeremenko (second from right) doing the work of all good field commanders – planning with a map. (Elukka)

Second Army moved out, XXIV Panzer Corps had slipped behind the defenders and cut off any escape. Remnants of the 21st Army evacuated the city on August 17 and the Germans occupied it two days later, rounding up another 50,000 POWs.

Guderian reached Starodub on August 18. After occupying the town the Germans sent bogus transmissions to Timoshenko's headquarters to the effect that the Red Army still held it and warning against bombing it.

On August 20, Stalin ordered Yeremenko to destroy Guderian. Yeremenko employed the 13th (once again) and 50th Armies plus elements of the badly beaten 3rd and 21st, but failed to halt the Panzers. The dictator told Yeremenko "Stavka is much displeased with your work;" but except for three divisions facing XXXV Army Corps in the Rokitno Marshes, the Central Front had ceased to exist.

The Germans' road to the south now lay wide open. The Second Army continued down the Gomel–Chernigov highway in late August. XIII, XLIII and XXXV Army Corps assaulted Chernigov on the lower Desna with air support; Red Army troops set fire to it and withdrew on the night of September 6–7. (Guderian's push toward the Kiev encirclement is related in the first part of this trilogy, Campaign 129.)

In Hitler's mind the *Kessel* at Gomel and the plunge southward by Second Panzer Group and Second Army were logical stepping-stones toward Kiev. At the end of July, as Smolensk and its ancillary battles were being cleaned up, Von Bock had tempting targets 200 miles east (Moscow) and 200 miles south (the Southwest Front); but, as related, the German senior command indulged in a time-wasting contest of wills, particularly between Hitler and Halder. German strategic thinking could not keep pace with the fast-moving Panzer formations on the battlefield; but German moves confirmed Soviet thinking that proved to be just as mistaken. Hoth's and Guderian's drives north and south appeared to them as evidence of Von Bock's natural desire to firm up his flanks prior to the final frontal assault on their capital. To that end they made Yelnia a symbol at the door to Moscow.

Adapt and overcome: the German 8.8cm Flak 18 gun changed roles and became famous throughout the European theater as the ultimate direct fire antitank weapon. (HITM)

OCTOBER: OPERATION *TYPHOON*

In September, Army Group North arrived in the suburbs of Leningrad and severed the city from land communications. At Kiev, Army Group South, with the help of Second Army and Second Panzer Group, won history's greatest encirclement battle: two-thirds of a million men were trapped in a *Kessel* the size of Belgium, and the *Ostheer* outnumbered the Red Army for the first and only time in World War II. The Germans had paid a price, but to most of the world it looked as if the campaign would continue to go their way; their victory at Moscow was assumed.

Planning for *Typhoon*

For once the German leadership anticipated events, and Hitler issued his order for the final assault on Moscow almost ten days before the trap around the Southwest Front slammed shut at Lochvitsa. On September 6 his Directive No.35 stated that the successes of the flanking army groups had created the "prerequisites for conducting a decisive operation against Army Group Timoshenko, which is conducting unsuccessful offensive operations against Army Group Center's front." Hitler went on to instruct Von Bock to launch an operation against Army Group Timoshenko as quickly as possible "so that we can go on the offensive in the general direction of Viazma and destroy the enemy in the region east of Smolensk by double envelopment... After destroying the main mass of Timoshenko's group of forces in decisive encirclement and destruction operations, Army Group Center will begin pursuing enemy forces along the Moscow axes."

The OKH staff added its Directive for the Continuation of Operations four days later. Von Bock's staff had shelved a plan to attack Moscow because of the Kiev operation. On September 16 he issued his *Typhoon* operations order for three Panzer groups; Guderian would come back to him after concluding the Kiev operations, and from Army Group North he would later receive ColGen Erich Hoepner's Fourth Panzer Group (XXXXI & LVI Panzer Corps, totaling three armored, two motorized and two infantry divisions). As on *Barbarossatag*, Von Bock paired the Panzer

The Germans seriously underestimated the Communist Party's ability to mobilize the Soviet population to repel the invader. Here men and women dig an antitank ditch in front of Moscow. (Elukka)

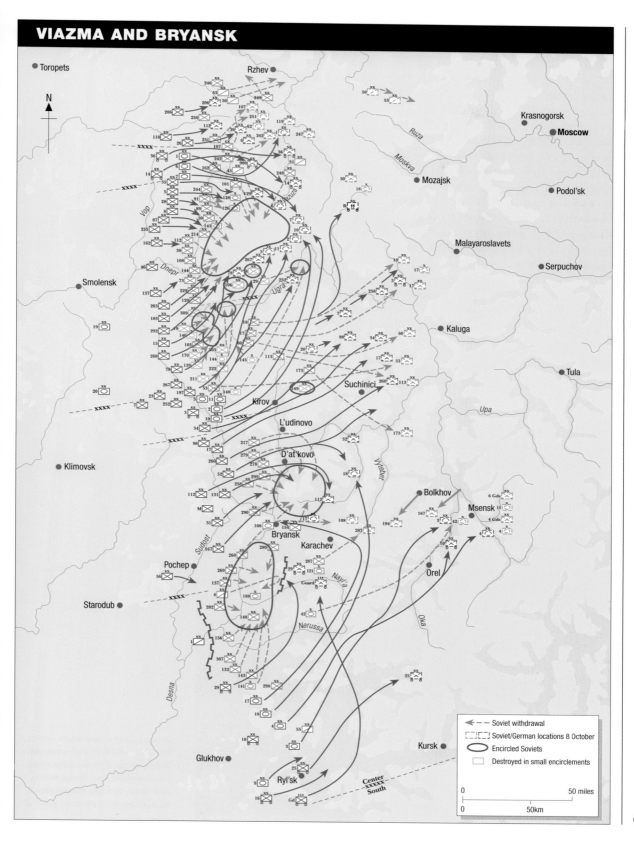

Toropets

N

Rzhev

Krasnogorsk

Moscow

Mozajsk

Podol'sk

Smolensk

Malayaroslavets

Serpuchov

Kaluga

Tula

Suchinici

Kirov

L'udinovo

Upa

D'at'kovo

Klimovsk

Bolkhov

Msensk

6 Gds

4 Gds

Bryansk

Karachev

Pochep

Orel

Starodub

Glukhov

Kursk

Ryl'sk

Center
XXXXX
South

Soviet withdrawal

Soviet/German locations 8 October

Encircled Soviets

Destroyed in small encirclements

0 ——————— 50 miles

0 ——————— 50km

67

Groups with field armies to ensure better coordination. *Typhoon*'s mission was to destroy the West, Reserve and Bryansk Fronts, and to prevent the enemy from retreating in good order to Moscow.

As usual, there was disagreement. Von Bock wanted a deeper encirclement east of Viazma, while OKH favored a shallower one aimed at that city. After closing the pockets Halder wanted to send the motorized units into Moscow, but Hitler wanted no part of urban combat, as he had made clear earlier at Kiev and Leningrad. Also, attempts to co-ordinate with an attack by Von Leeb toward Lake Il'men with Sixteenth Army, and with a movement by Von Rundstedt on Kharkov with Sixth Army, met with mixed results.

For a month now Army Group Center had fought a relatively static battle, so it had accurate tactical intelligence on Soviet strength and dispositions; it identified 80 of the 83 Soviet rifle divisions to its front (typically, FHO identified only 54 of them.) Even in this static situation, German logistics were still unsatisfactory: despite large depots at Gomel, Roslavl, Smolensk and Toropets they could only sustain a short burst towards Moscow. Panzer serviceability rates were also a problem: they stood at 50 percent for Guderian, 70–80 percent for Hoth, and 100 percent only for Hoepner. Prior to *Typhoon* 4th Panzer Division, for example, received as replacements only 30 PzKpfw IIIs and five PzKpfw IVs (for a total of 110 operational tanks), and only enough fuel to travel 60 miles.

With Von Brauchitsch, Halder and Kesselring in attendance, Von Bock hosted a conference on September 24 to wargame *Typhoon* with his subordinate commanders. Fourth Army and Fourth Panzer Group in the center represented *Typhoon*'s *Schwerpunkt*. Not wanting to take any chances on the weather, Guderian obtained permission to begin his assault two days early. Most subordinate commands issued their orders on the 26th. For *Typhoon*, Army Group Center mustered 1,929,000 soldiers in 56 infantry, 14 armored and eight motorized divisions; together they counted 14,000 indirect-fire weapons and 1,000 tanks, and the Luftwaffe contributed 1,390 aircraft.

A busy scene, complete with a halted Panzer III and a convoy led by a quad 2cm Flakvierling cannon mounted on an SdKfz 7/1 halftrack, followed by trucks, motorcycles, staff cars and other vehicles. (HITM)

Soviet preparations

The Soviets would soon regret expending so much energy in attacking during late summer. On September 10, four days after the issue of Führer Directive 35, Stavka ordered forces facing Von Bock to take up the defense. By then the average strength of many rifle divisions stood at only about 3,000 men. Since mid-July the Soviets had been building and improving works to defend their capital. The most important of these, the Mozhaisk Line, was 40–50 percent complete by September 30, and the same could be said for the other three Fortified Regions: Volokolamsk, Maloyaroslavets and Kaluga. The Soviets had expected the "final assault" on Moscow around late August, and had allowed themselves to be lulled into a false sense of security since then. But they also assumed, given the imminent season of *rasputitsa* (rain and mud), that Hitler would not try to attack following the Kiev battle. Further, they thought that most of the German armor was in the north and south. Red Army intelligence missed the movement of much of Fourth Panzer Group from Von Leeb to Von Bock, and the return of Second Panzer Group plus some of Von Kleist's First Panzer Group.

Stavka knew that after Kiev there would be no more trading space for time before Moscow. However, with a mistaken appreciation of the correlation of forces, it is no surprise that they also defended the wrong places. They expected the main thrust directly at Viazma along the Minsk highway. Von Bock's strikes on either side of the main defenses, and Guderian's thrust south of Bryansk, caught them completely off guard. As one post-Soviet Russian history put it: "Stavka failed to divine the German intentions... it issued its warning of an impending attack too late, and when it did, it never ordered the Reserve Front to prepare its defenses."

From north to south, ColGen Konev commanded the West Front (22nd, 29th, 30th, 19th, 16th & 20th Armies) along a line 210 miles long. Budenny's Reserve Front (24th & 43rd Armies) guarded 60 miles of the

Early July: a Nebelwerfer battery with 7th Panzer Division preparing to fire. Projectiles can be seen protruding from the rear of the launcher's lower tubes. Note that the crewmen are wearing protective overalls. (NARA)

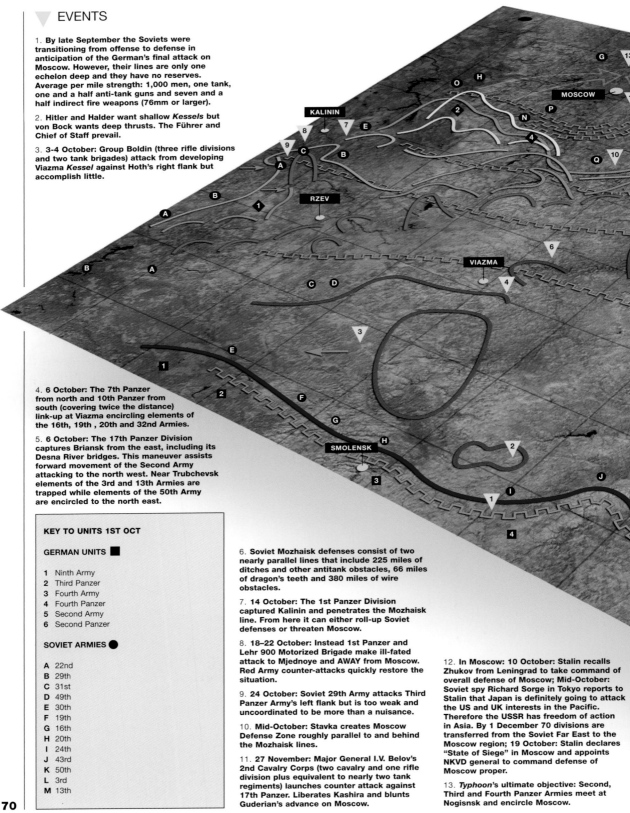

▼ EVENTS

1. **By late September the Soviets were transitioning from offense to defense in anticipation of the German's final attack on Moscow. However, their lines are only one echelon deep and they have no reserves. Average per mile strength: 1,000 men, one tank, one and a half anti-tank guns and seven and a half indirect fire weapons (76mm or larger).**

2. Hitler and Halder want shallow *Kessels* but von Bock wants deep thrusts. The Führer and Chief of Staff prevail.

3. **3–4 October: Group Boldin (three rifle divisions and two tank brigades) attack from developing Viazma *Kessel* against Hoth's right flank but accomplish little.**

4. **6 October: The 7th Panzer from north and 10th Panzer from south (covering twice the distance) link-up at Viazma encircling elements of the 16th, 19th , 20th and 32nd Armies.**

5. **6 October: The 17th Panzer Division captures Briansk from the east, including its Desna River bridges. This maneuver assists forward movement of the Second Army attacking to the north west. Near Trubchevsk elements of the 3rd and 13th Armies are trapped while elements of the 50th Army are encircled to the north east.**

KEY TO UNITS 1ST OCT

GERMAN UNITS ■

1 Ninth Army
2 Third Panzer
3 Fourth Army
4 Fourth Panzer
5 Second Army
6 Second Panzer

SOVIET ARMIES ●

A 22nd
B 29th
C 31st
D 49th
E 30th
F 19th
G 16th
H 20th
I 24th
J 43rd
K 50th
L 3rd
M 13th

6. **Soviet Mozhaisk defenses consist of two nearly parallel lines that include 225 miles of ditches and other antitank obstacles, 66 miles of dragon's teeth and 380 miles of wire obstacles.**

7. **14 October: The 1st Panzer Division captured Kalinin and penetrates the Mozhaisk line. From here it can either roll-up Soviet defenses or threaten Moscow.**

8. **18–22 October: Instead 1st Panzer and Lehr 900 Motorized Brigade make ill-fated attack to Mjednoye and AWAY from Moscow. Red Army counter-attacks quickly restore the situation.**

9. **24 October: Soviet 29th Army attacks Third Panzer Army's left flank but is too weak and uncoordinated to be more than a nuisance.**

10. **Mid-October: Stavka creates Moscow Defense Zone roughly parallel to and behind the Mozhaisk lines.**

11. **27 November: Major General I.V. Belov's 2nd Cavalry Corps (two cavalry and one rifle division plus equivalent to nearly two tank regiments) launches counter attack against 17th Panzer. Liberates Kashira and blunts Guderian's advance on Moscow.**

12. **In Moscow: 10 October: Stalin recalls Zhukov from Leningrad to take command of overall defense of Moscow; Mid-October: Soviet spy Richard Sorge in Tokyo reports to Stalin that Japan is definitely going to attack the US and UK interests in the Pacific. Therefore the USSR has freedom of action in Asia. By 1 December 70 divisions are transferred from the Soviet Far East to the Moscow region; 19 October: Stalin declares "State of Siege" in Moscow and appoints NKVD general to command defense of Moscow proper.**

13. **_Typhoon_'s ultimate objective: Second, Third and Fourth Panzer Armies meet at Nogisnsk and encircle Moscow.**

OPERATION *TYPHOON*

After securing their northern and southern flanks the Germans were ready for *Barbarossa*'s culminating event, the assault on Moscow. After having been successful everywhere for the preceding four months the Ostheer had no reason to think Operation *Typhoon* would not likewise meet all expectations. A small, fanatical group at the top of the Soviet leadership believed they could halt the onslaught.

Note: Gridlines are shown at intervals of 51km/31miles

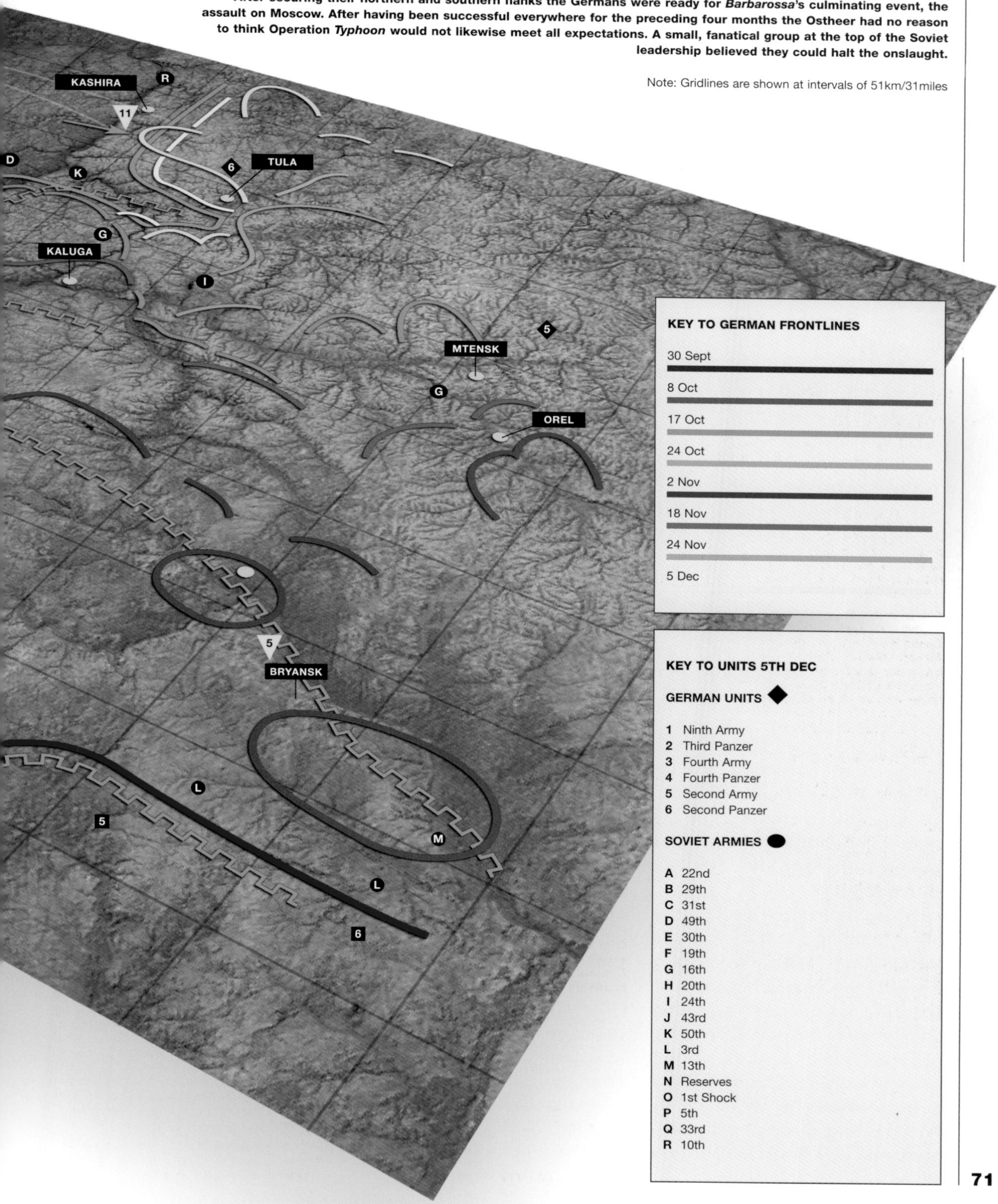

KASHIRA R
11
D
K
6 TULA
G
KALUGA
I
5
MTENSK
G
OREL
5
BRYANSK
L
5
M
L
6

KEY TO GERMAN FRONTLINES

30 Sept

8 Oct

17 Oct

24 Oct

2 Nov

18 Nov

24 Nov

5 Dec

KEY TO UNITS 5TH DEC

GERMAN UNITS ◆

1 Ninth Army
2 Third Panzer
3 Fourth Army
4 Fourth Panzer
5 Second Army
6 Second Panzer

SOVIET ARMIES ●

A 22nd
B 29th
C 31st
D 49th
E 30th
F 19th
G 16th
H 20th
I 24th
J 43rd
K 50th
L 3rd
M 13th
N Reserves
O 1st Shock
P 5th
Q 33rd
R 10th

front, while his 31st, 49th, 32nd & 33rd Armies stood to the rear. On the southern flank, Yeremenko's Bryansk Front (50th, 3rd & 13th Armies plus Operational Group Ermakov) covered 180 miles. Many of these armies had been fighting since June 22, and their headquarters had been encircled and/or escaped encirclement many times. Owing to losses incurred at Viazma–Bryansk (see below) many of the defending units would be militia divisions, although some of them had been fighting since Yelnia.

Logistics problems also plagued the Red Army. Ammunition, transport and repair capacity, fuel and aviation gas had all been used up during the "Timoshenko Offensive." Many *frontoviki* lacked winter clothing – it was not only the Germans who failed in this regard. However, while Von Bock had literally no reserves for *Typhoon*, at least the "beaten" Red Army had husbanded some.

Fully 40 percent of the entire Red Army between Leningrad and the Black Sea defended Moscow: 1,250,000 men (including 193,000 new soldiers) manned 83 rifle, 2 mechanized, one tank and nine cavalry divisions plus 13 tank brigades. Sixty-six rifle divisions occupied the first echelon, with 17 rifle divisions and seven tank brigades behind them, and 12 rifle divisions and six tank brigades stood in reserve. They were supported by 7,600 guns, 990 tanks, and 863 aircraft (perhaps two-thirds of them operational).

On September 26, Konev reported that the Germans were preparing to attack across his front on October 1. This news completely surprised Stalin, who issued another defensive directive the next day. By the end of September the Soviets were confident that their system could respond, survive, and probably not collapse. On the other hand, so far the Germans had always succeeded.

Viazma and Bryansk

"Fast Heinz" Guderian lived up to his nickname when he moved out on September 30, two days before the rest of Army Group Center. Outside the ancient Ukrainian capital of Glukhov he hit the unprepared Operational Group Ermakov and scattered its five divisions, soon creating a 13-mile gap between him and 13th Army. Ermakov rallied his forces to counterattack a day later, but did not have much impact because of the usual failings: poor co-ordination, too few tanks and no air support. However, by nightfall 3rd Panzer Division had its first experience with *Katyusha* rockets, dogs trained to run under tanks with explosives fixed to their backs, and almost undetectable wooden-cased, antitank mines.

Since the rest of the front seemed to be quiet, Yeremenko and the high command considered Guderian's assault a diversion. (Fog and rain limited Luftwaffe activity, further deceiving the defenders.) Nevertheless, Stavka began moving reserves toward the point of rupture (because of Guderian's reputation?); they were soon to find that the real danger lay to the north. To complicate matters they had no clear picture of events, since Luftwaffe raids cut Yeremenko's communications.

On October 2, Ninth and Fourth Armies created penetrations in the Soviet defenses in trench-fighting involving bayonets, hand grenades, sidearms and spades; by the end of that day 260th Infantry Division had overcome 120 bunkers. The infantry often reoccupied the same Yelnia battlefields that they had given up a month earlier. Hoth's and Hoepner's armor exploited through the gaps, and it took the latter only two hours to overcome the River Desna defenses. The 7th Panzer Division's artillery preparation amounted to 130 tubes per mile, while their 300 tanks spread across a one-and-a-half-mile front in two waves. Third Panzer Group split 19th and 30th Armies apart, while the Fourth Panzer smashed 43rd Army in Budenny's first echelon and hit the 33rd Army behind it. Hoth's men were supported by four fighter and attack Geschwader.

Within 24 hours Von Kluge began to interfere by ordering Hoepner, 50 miles into the Soviet rear, to redirect XLVI Panzer Corps northward in order to create a smaller encirclement west of Viazma – yet another dangerous dispersion of armor that was intended to be employed in mass. The bulk of Fourth Panzer Group raced up the road toward Yukhnov, including 5th Panzer Division (new to the theater, and originally earmarked for Africa, so many of its vehicles still wore their desert paint scheme). Soviet fighter pilots reported this movement, but Marshal Shaposhnikov demanded repeated confirmation, and by the time he received it the town had already fallen.

Logistics reared its ugly head when, after breaking into Konev's second-echelon 32nd Army, Hoth literally ran out of fuel on October 4, and his spearhead required Luftwaffe resupply; he could not move again until the 5th. Konev used that small pause to request permission to retreat from the quickly developing trap; he later commented, "Stalin listened to me, but made no decision." He therefore ordered a relief assault toward Viazma against the German flanks, by Boldin from the north and Rokossovsky's 16th Army from the south. That night Stavka allowed Konev to begin retreating out of the encirclement. (In an unrelated event, Hoth had now left for Army Group South to command Seventeenth Army, and ColGen Hans-Georg Reinhardt took command of his Third Panzer Group.)

The following morning Konev told 16th and 19th Armies to exfiltrate eastward, an order repeated to the rest of the West Front on October 7; and he ordered Rokossovsky – unrealistically – to hold Viazma. These measures were too late: on the morning of the 7th, Reinhardt's 7th Panzer Division met Hoepner's 10th Panzer at Viazma. General Lukin, who had only escaped from Smolensk two months earlier, was now placed in charge of forces inside the Viazma pocket, with the mission of breaking out during

The terrible mud of the *rasputitsa* season affected all equally. Here soldiers and civilians (note the woman in a skirt, left) man-handle a Soviet supply truck which has got itself stuck axle deep. (Podzun)

the night of October 10–11 toward Gzhatsk, through the weak 11th Panzer Division cordon.

In the south, the original mission of Second Army was to cover Von Kluge's right flank and let Guderian trap Yeremenko. But, as before at Minsk and Smolensk, Guderian cared less about closing off encirclements than driving east. He remained focused on Moscow, without worrying about his exposed flanks – the Southwest Front to his right was too weak after Kiev to mount a serious threat. Von Weichs's slowness and Guderian's neglect conspired to slow the Bryansk half of the triple envelopment. Eventually Second Army picked up its pace, and Guderian finally sent his XLVII Panzer Corps (17th & 18th Panzer Divisions) around the east side of Bryansk. On October 5 the tanks cut the rail connection from Moscow, the front's lifeline; the next day they almost captured the Bryansk Front headquarters (Yeremenko and his adjutant escaped); and two days later they linked up with Second Army north of the city. The second, incomplete *Kessel* had closed.

At Viazma and Bryansk the Germans destroyed seven of 15 Soviet armies, 64 of 95 divisions, 11 of 15 tank brigades and 50 of 62 artillery regiments. They listed 6,000 guns and mortars and 830 tanks destroyed, killed approximately 332,000 Red Army soldiers, and marched 668,000 into captivity. However, the walls of the German trap were porous: approximately 85,000 men escaped from Viazma and another 23,000 from Bryansk. Although they had lost their heavy weapons, these men – plus another 100,000 escapees from 22nd, 29th & 33rd Armies and Group Ermakov – lived to fight another day, and trickled east to occupy Moscow's various defensive positions.

Until November

Von Bock issued his order for the continuation of operations on October 7. In the north, Ninth Army and Third Panzer Group would advance on Rzhev and Kalinin; in the center Fourth Army would make for Maloyaroslavets and Kaluga, while Hoepner aimed for Mozhaisk; to the

Civilians and soldiers formed many militia divisions for the urgent defense of large Soviet cities. It is likely that these men, photographed in the shadow of Moscow's Kremlin walls, are heading directly out to the fighting line; note their mixture of uniform and civilian clothing. (Elukka)

south, Guderian (his command now renamed Second Panzer Army) would drive on towards Tula with Second Army in support. However, all this had to wait until the two encirclements were cleared, a task requiring two-thirds of the army group and between one and two weeks. Additionally, Army Group Center's logistic woes prevented it from continuing sustained operations. So, just when Von Bock had rent a 300-mile hole in the Moscow defenses, behind which the Soviets could muster scant reserves, he had to slow down to await reduction of the two pockets and to reconsolidate his army group.

Stage II of *Typhoon* also had to contend with worsening weather. Rain began to fall in the southern sector on October 6 and elsewhere a day later. Luftwaffe sorties dropped from 1,400 on October 6–7 to 139 on the 9th. Supplies could not come forward, and the wounded could not be evacuated. Nevertheless, that same day Halder was optimistic about the chances of encircling Moscow. For a few hours those odds lengthened dramatically, as Hitler toyed with the idea of sending Guderian and Von Weichs south toward Kursk. Although he scrapped the idea within hours, this is further proof of the minimal importance the dictator placed on Moscow, and the corresponding value he attached to destroying the Red Army. After all, many German leaders assumed that they had eliminated Soviet forces defending Moscow at Viazma and Bryansk, and should therefore concentrate on the flanks.

Simultaneously in the Kremlin, Zhukov told Stavka that "the chief danger is that all routes to Moscow are open and the weak protection along the Mozhaisk line cannot guarantee against the surprise appearance of enemy armored forces before Moscow." Having just arrived from Leningrad, he recommended massing all available forces along the Mozhaisk. The Soviet high command therefore created the Moscow Reserve Front under Moscow Military District commander LtGen P.A. Artemev, to hold the positions Zhukov suggested – now determined to be Moscow's principal line of defense.

A captured Soviet GAZ-AAA truck perseveres through muddy conditions in autumn 1941. Trucks such as these were captured by German troops frequently, and they coped with difficult terrain better than most German vehicles. (Nik Cornish at Stavka)

The crew of a 2cm Flak gun build a fire to keep warm while guarding a bridge near Mozhaisk. As often happened, retreating Soviets demolished the original bridge, only for German engineers to build another right next to it. (Author's collection)

On October 10, Third Panzer Group moved toward Kalinin with the Ninth Army covering its left. Their mission was to join up, lever the Northwest Front off the Moscow–Leningrad railway, then turn southeast against the capital itself. The defending 22nd and 29th Armies put up a good initial defense, but 1st Panzer Division entered Kalinin on October 14. From here Reinhardt could turn right and either initiate a deep encirclement of Moscow, or roll up the Mozhaisk line.

It took Northwest Front Chief of Staff N.F. Vatutin one day to organize a counterattack force of two rifle and two cavalry divisions plus a tank brigade, but fighting lasted two full weeks as both sides poured units into the battle. By the end of October neither had the energy to go farther. VIII Fliegerkorps occupied recently abandoned airfields around Kalinin, only to see them blasted by Soviet artillery. Meanwhile Zhukov dispatched Konev to command the new Kalinin Front, which basically connected that city with Moscow along the Volga.

On the old Napoleonic battlefield at Borodino two regiments of the newly arrived Siberian 32nd Rifle Division plus 18th and 19th Tank Brigades tried to halt 10th Panzer and SS "Reich" Divisions. On one night the commander of a company from 98th Infantry Division requested permission to attack. "Attack where?", the regiment asked; the lieutenant answered, "We're freezing – it doesn't matter where, we need quarters!"

Due west of Moscow, Army Group Center assaulted the new Moscow Reserve Front, specifically 16th Army at Volokolomsk, 5th Army at Mozhaisk, 43rd Army at Maloyaroslavets and 49th Army at Kaluga. By October 16 all four had been defeated. These setbacks could have meant the end of the Moscow defenses, but instead the Soviet resistance stiffened. In about ten days during mid-October the forces defending the Mozhaisk positions grew from six rifle divisions, a like number of tank brigades and ten artillery regiments, to 14 rifle divisions, 16 tank brigades and over 40 artillery regiments. These defenses were not simply a single line but reached in depth all the way to Moscow. With the Luftwaffe expending little effort on interdiction since mid-October, the capital's railway system provided an easy way to reinforce the Mozhaisk positions.

Part way through the battle Stavka merged Artemev's command with the West Front. On the southern flank, Guderian's progress slowed dramatically when XXIV Panzer Corps ran out of fuel, and was then stopped completely at Mtsensk by the 1st Guards Rifle Corps. After Kiev, parts of the Second Army, especially its rear services, were still struggling north during mid-October, so could not contribute fully in this sector. Luftwaffe Ju 52 transports refueled Guderian by dropping supplies, since they could not land in the mud. At the end of the month 60 men from "Grossdeutschland" shot their way into Tula, but were thrown out within hours, never to return. The southern edge of that city marked the temporary limit of Guderian's advance.

As of October 14, Von Bock still believed that there were no Soviet units defending Moscow. Inside the capital panic set in, despite directives signed by Stalin and Shaposhnikov on October 8 and 9. On the 12th the GKO (State Defense Committee) put Moscow under NKVD control. Additional militia and "destroyer" units (local defense and security) were raised, and 440,000 workers were armed. Some government agencies evacuated the city for points east, and foreign embassies were advised to leave as well. However, on October 19 Stalin issued a directive meant to halt the panic once and for all. In mid-July Hitler had boasted that Moscow "must disappear from the face of the earth;" three months later, Stalin resolved to stay put and defend his capital. Both dictators staked their all on the fate of the city.

Exhaustion set in on both sides, and the Mozhaisk line marked the end of *Typhoon*. After the encirclements at Viazma and Bryansk the *Ostheer* continued successfully to exert pressure on the Red Army defenses, but achieved no breakthroughs. Hitler could not bring himself to assault Moscow frontally through its primary defenses, such as they were, and vainly sought a decision on the flanks.

On the north, although Third Panzer Group's occupation of Kalinin caused consternation, the maneuver represented just another dilution of German efforts; the distances from Viazma to Kalinin and Viazma to Moscow were the same 120 miles, but the effects of going in two different directions were enormous. In the south, for the third time during *Barbarossa*, Guderian had put personal goals ahead of organizational ones – on this occasion by his sloppy completion of the Bryansk *Kessel* – and still he could not get appreciably closer to Moscow.

At the time and since, German commentators have used the autumn weather as an excuse for *Typhoon*'s failure, as if the *rasputitsa* was unpredictable. In fact, rainfall in 1941 was slightly below average for October, and less than 0.5in above average for November. The temperature in 1941 was only 2°(F) lower than the average for October, and 3.5°(F) colder for November. Conversely, the frost came a little early in 1941 – an advantage for the Germans. The wet and cold certainly did prevent a fast advance on Moscow after Viazma and Bryansk; but solid German staff work would have prepared the *Ostheer* better for the entirely predictable weather.

On the other side of the front, at Viazma and Bryansk Stalin rolled the dice for the third time, with results that his failures at Minsk and Smolensk made predictable. At each stop along the Moscow axis he had underestimated the speed and violence of the Blitzkrieg, while overestimating the benefits of standing fast in immobile defenses. Likewise, after four months of hard lessons the Red Army still could not mount effective counterattacks against German armored spearheads.

Soviet defenses toughened noticeably by the time the Red Army occupied the Mozhaisk positions. Zhukov knew that thanks to the weather he could concentrate along the few all-weather roads. Rumors were reaching the *frontoviki* about the treatment of earlier Red Army captives at the hands of the Wehrmacht, so surrender became completely unattractive. In mid-October (the exact date is unknown) Stalin heard from his master spy in Tokyo, Richard Sorge, that Japan would not help Germany against the USSR, but was heading south toward the Philippines and Indonesia. Soon one division from the Soviet Far East was arriving near Moscow by rail every two days; by the end of the month an additional 13 rifle divisions and five tank brigades were present. German intelligence failed completely to identify this build-up. Rastenburg, OKW and OKH simply could not believe that after Kiev, Viazma and Bryansk and all its other disasters the Red Army had anything left to put in their path before Moscow.

CLOSING IN ON MOSCOW

During the second half of October the Germans hoped to build upon the momentum of the Viazma–Bryansk offensive, but their own weaknesses, the weather and Soviet resistance made this impossible. Red Army forces along the entire front and in reserves close behind would grow from 269 divisions and 65 brigades totaling 2.2 million men at the beginning of November, to 343 divisions and 98 brigades with over 4 million men a month later – and most of these new troops manned the Moscow sectors. On November 1 Von Bock's forces fielded 136 divisions on paper, but with a real strength of 83, totaling 2.7 million men, and he would receive no reinforcements.

On the last day of the month OKH issued yet another "Continuation of Operations Directive." It ordered Ninth Army to attack toward the Volga Reservoir while Third and Fourth Panzer Groups would slash toward Yaroslavl (nearly 200 miles northeast of the Volga) in the north. Second Panzer Army, with only 50 of its 600 tanks operational, aimed for Gorky (over 200 miles distant), with Second Army covering its right while also making for Voronezh. Once again Fourth Army represented the army group's *Schwerpunkt*, with Moscow as its objective. The attack would begin on November 15. The other army groups received equally unrealistic missions: North was to link up with the Finns, while South was to push on to Stalingrad and Maikop!

Could Army Group Center reach Moscow? Von Bock had wanted it all along, and now he would have his way. Like most German officers of that time, he was almost terminally optimistic: his soldiers *would* win the final battle, he *would* follow Hitler's orders, and he *would* capture the legendary city.

Preliminaries

On November 6, marking the anniversary of the 1917 Revolution, Stalin told soldiers marching from Red Square directly to the battlefield, "If they want a war of extermination, they shall have one." He feared the Germans could encircle Leningrad, Moscow, Rostov and Stalingrad and perhaps even capture them. He therefore reinforced Zhukov's West

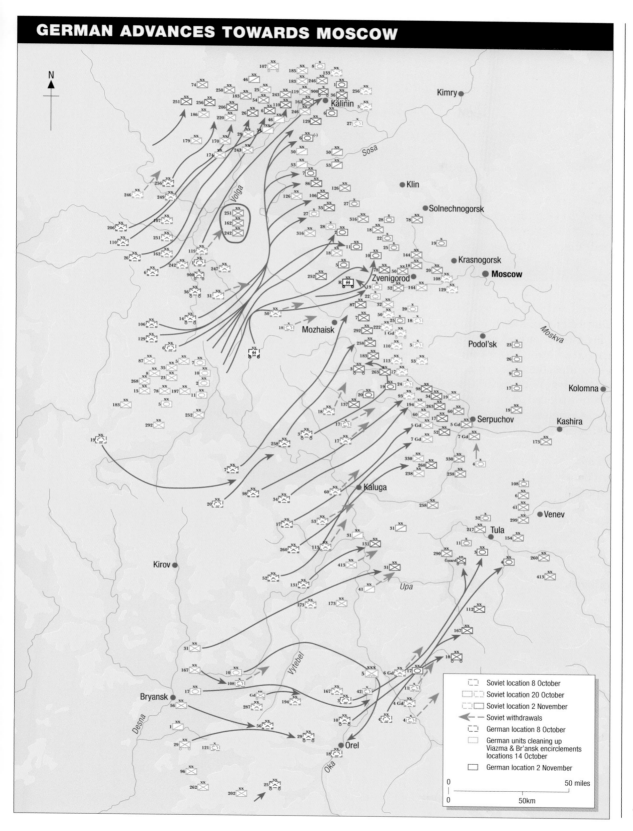

Legend:

- Soviet location 8 October
- Soviet location 20 October
- Soviet location 2 November
- Soviet withdrawals
- German location 8 October
- German units cleaning up Viazma & Br'ansk encirclements locations 14 October
- German location 2 November

0 — 50 miles
0 — 50km

Gaining the upper hand: emboldened by flagging German fortunes, and motivated to defend their capital, the Soviets increased their offensive activity in November and December. Here T-34/76 tanks accompany advancing Red Army infantrymen. (Elukka)

Front, supported by Konev's Kalinin Front to the north and Timoshenko's Southwest Front in the south.

Zhukov wanted control of the entire battle for Moscow, and Stalin gave it to him. The West Front took command of 50th Army (from the disbanded Bryansk Front) on November 10, and 13th Army at Kalinin a week later. With fresh lessons from the defense of Leningrad in mind, Stalin ordered Zhukov to launch a series of pre-emptive assaults against the Germans; the general argued against this plan, but ultimately followed orders.

On the left, 49th Army (LtGen I.G. Zakharkin) attacked on November 14 against XII and XIII Army Corps near Serpukhov; 2nd Cavalry Corps tried to exploit, but failed to have much impact. Two days later, near Volokolamsk, Rokossovsky led his 16th Army into the gap between 14th Motorized and 7th Panzer Divisions, likewise achieving little success. New units from the Far East had little time to prepare, were unused to combat, and lost up to one-third of their personnel and 157 of 198 tanks in ill-advised assaults. The follow-on charge of MajGen L.M. Dovator's 3rd Cavalry Corps was essentially suicidal; his 44th Cavalry Division practically ceased to exist, and its sister 17th had 75 percent casualties. These attacks severely weakened Red Army forces that would soon desperately need all their available strength; however, merely taking the offensive bolstered Soviet confidence.

On the day before Zhukov's first attacks, Halder met with most of the *Ostheer*'s army and army group chiefs of staff at Orsha. He arrived unable to imagine that the Red Army had any means left to stop Von Bock before Moscow, but German intelligence was so poor they had no way to confirm or deny their assumptions. With Moscow now so close, the historic city was exerting an allure over many German leaders. Halder "hoped" for six more weeks of cold weather without much snow.

His hopes were dashed by the men who had just come from the fighting front. Von Bock's chief of staff, Von Greiffenberg, echoed his commander when he said that Moscow could only be taken frontally, and that Halder's grandiose encirclements were out of the question. Halder conceded, and allowed the less ambitious army group plan to go forward.

A combination of ancient and modern: German supplies are offloaded from a Ju 52 trimotor transport aircraft and onto a horse-drawn *panje* sled. Distance, weather, terrain and partisan activity made aerial resupply essential on many occasions, but this was a task for which the Luftwaffe was inadequately equipped. Meanwhile, the Red Army was also using air transport: Stalin had flown 5,500 men of 1st Guards Rifle Corps to Orel in just three days. (Podzun)

Kesselring spoke up to say that many of his Luftwaffe units had already left for the Mediterranean, and that his staff and "a substantial number of units" would depart on November 18. As usual, logistics concerns were soon being voiced. The OKH quartermaster representative said that they could not supply the army group; for example, fuel deliveries were one-quarter of requirements. Halder's response to this real problem was simply to announce that OKH was "not going to stand in Von Bock's way if he thinks he can succeed; you also need a little bit of luck in war." Even though rail lines had operated to Gzhatsk by October 27 and to Borodino a few days later, Von Bock's logistics remained under stress, causing the staggered start of his final push. Nevertheless, Army Group Center wanted to start as soon as possible; only Moscow justified this risk.

There would be few modifications to the plan of attack. Owing to the dire situation of Von Leeb's Sixteenth Army to the north, Ninth Army's mission was limited. Reinhardt's Third Panzer Group would attack on November 15 and aim for the Volga–Moscow Canal. Three days later, Hoepner's Fourth Panzer Group and Guderian's Second Panzer Army would move out toward Teryayevo and Kolomna respectively. Von Kluge, whose Fourth Army should have had major responsibilities, was left in limbo. The Second Army had to accomplish the impossible combination of covering the flanks of the Fourth and Second Panzer Armies, while maintaining contact with the Sixth Army of Army Group South, and also conducting its own attacks on Orel, Kursk and Voronezh.

Army Group Center received no reinforcements to make up its losses from combat and illness; meanwhile, the Soviets around Moscow received 100,000 men, 300 tanks and 2,000 guns during the first half of November alone. Among the new formations was an Engineer Army with 19 pioneer battalions to help Zhukov dig in. Now, along the main front, 233,000 Germans, with 1,880 guns, 1,300 tanks and approximately 800 aircraft were facing 240,000 Soviet soldiers, 1,254 guns, 502 tanks and 1,238 aircaft. While Halder wrote on November 5 that "the Luftwaffe is slowly disintegrating" on its primitive frontline airstrips, most Red Army Air Force squadrons were operating from the well-equipped permanent airfields surrounding Moscow.

137TH INFANTRY DIVISION ASSAULT THROUGH THE MOSCOW DEFENSES NEAR VORONINO, NOVEMBER 17, 1941

(pages 82–83)

In August and September, Hitler had opted for firming up *Barbarossa*'s flanks while destroying huge numbers of Red Army forces; Moscow had to wait. In October, Operation *Typhoon* began with great promise, but then bogged down in the autumn rains and mud – the *rasputitsa*. The freezing weather of November added new miseries for soldiers of both sides, but at least it allowed continued German forward movement.

Barbarossa's last lunge would have to fight its way through hand-dug fortifications, Stavka's last thrown-together reserves, and units newly arriving from the Soviet Far East. Despite heavy casualties and sheer exhaustion, neither side showed any sign of letting up. After marching nearly a thousand kilometers, the long-suffering German infantry would find the last hundred to Moscow among the hardest. Hitler, Halder and most of the Reich leadership expected glorious victory to await them in Stalin's capital; and while the *Landser* fought for each new village mostly in hope of finding shelter from the next freezing night, the thought of Moscow did exert a powerful attraction. At the far end of a long and poorly-executed logistic tail, they did find some ammunition trickling forward, but in terms of food, fodder and clothing it was often a case of every man for himself.

Defending their capital also motivated the Red Army. The massive *Kessel* battles of summer and autumn had swallowed up two whole waves of armies; the third and last – a combination of militiamen, barely-trained levies and untried troops from the Far East – would fight behind three main lines of defenses, mostly built by Moscow's civilians under the harsh supervision of the Communist Party and NKVD. Soviet logistic problems eased as the front lines approached Moscow, with reinforcements and equipment going directly from the arriving trains to the front lines in a few hours.

This scene shows infantry (1) and engineers (2) of the 137th Infantry Division negotiating the defenses near Voronino almost due south of Moscow, between Maloyaroslavets and Serphukov. The infantry first fought their way across a steep-sided antitank ditch and then through the primitive earthen field works beyond, losing many men to mines and machine-gun fire. The Soviets quickly launched counterattacks, often supported by tanks (3). Early on November 17, Soviet tanks overran two howitzers; the divisional commander, General Bergmann, asked for reinforcements, in this case 8.8cm Flak 36 guns of Corps Flak Abteilung 707 (4), pulled by their SdKfz prime movers (5) over a tactical bridge erected by the engineers (6). Overhead, Nebelwerfer rockets pound the Soviet lines (7).

While undoubtedly still very cold, well-clothed Red Army infantry march across open terrain. In these near whiteout conditions the horizon where earth and sky meet is indistinguishable. (Elukka)

Von Bock versus Zhukov: North

Operation *Volga Reservoir* began on November 15, with Ninth Army's XXVII Army Corps joined by Third Panzer Group's LVI Panzer Corps and Hoepner's V and XLVI Army Corps a day later. (It took Strauss until the 20th to relieve Reinhardt's XLI Panzer Corps, which was still defending Kalinin and so could not participate in the attack.) They made good progress, all things considered, and reached both the reservoir and the canal to Moscow on the 18th. When VII and IX Army and XL Panzer Corps threw their weight into the battle Rokossovsky's situation became desperate. Von Bock's special command train moved to his army group's northern flank in anticipation of continued progress.

The 16th Army commander requested permission from Zhukov to withdraw to the Istra river, but was refused. Rokossovsky then went over his Front commander's head and made the same request of Chief of Staff Shaposhnikov, who authorized the retreat. Zhukov sent a stinging telegram to his subordinate countermanding any withdrawal. Thereafter Zhukov ruled with iron discipline. (He had the commander and commissar of 133rd Rifle Division executed in front of their troops for allowing an unauthorized retreat.)

Remnants of Dovator's cavalry corps managed to slow Hoepner, but Reinhardt made good progress against the boundary between 16th and 30th Armies. Third Panzer Group hit the right flank of 5th Army (now under Gen L.A. Govorov) near Zvenigorod on November 19–20. On the 21st, Zhukov sent Rokossovsky and the 16th Army deputy commander to personally shore up the situations at Solnechnogorsk and Klin respectively. Solnechnogorsk fell before Rokossovsky arrived, so both generals went to Klin – which fell anyway on the 22nd.

Zhukov's right threatened to become unhinged when 30th Army swung north, creating a gap that Reinhardt soon exploited. Stalin dispatched all reserves, including all air assets, to the northern sector. The XLI (commanded by Model) and XLVI Panzer Corps crossed the frozen Istra Reservoir during the last days of November. Army Group Center's farthest advance north of Moscow occurred on November 27, when Col Hasso von Manteuffel of 7th Panzer Division (now down to

Weather not fit for man nor beast: a small German supply column, including a "goulash cannon" field kitchen, makes its way past a knocked-out T-34. During winter raids, Soviet troops often targeted these trailers; in 1939–40 they had learned the hard way from the Finns that the combat potential of an isolated unit without the means to provide hot food and drink would degrade overnight. (HITM)

36 operational tanks) captured a bridgehead over the Volga at Yakhroma.

The 1st Shock Army – which the Soviets had been secretly building out of seven rifle brigades and 11 ski battalions, for another mission – was thrown into the breach between 16th and 30th Armies against the Third Panzer Group bridgehead. With only one very weak armored corps able to make it this far, the Germans gave up their Yakhroma outpost on the 29th. Another German outfit made it even closer to the Soviet capital when 2nd Panzer Division captured Krasnaya Polyana, only 12 miles from the Kremlin. The combination of 1st Shock and 20th Armies (the latter commanded by the brilliant but traitorous A.A. Vlassov) halted this threat as well. On 3 December, Hoepner called for a three-day halt; but before the Germans could get started again the Soviet general counteroffensive had begun.

Von Bock versus Zhukov: South

A less serious threat developed to the south of Moscow when Guderian's Second Panzer Army attacked toward Tula on November 18. He initially made good progress, causing a 30-mile gap along the boundary of the West and Southwest Fronts, but his men soon came up against new Siberian divisions that Guderian described as "keen for battle and well trained." By the 22nd he wanted to stop on account of extended flanks, terrible weather, high casualties, poor logistics and many other problems. The following day Von Bock flew to Guderian's headquarters to prop up his flagging subordinate and urge the Second Panzer Army to continue at least as far as Kolomna. But when Guderian hit Tula, "little Moscow," defended by a hodgepodge of workers' brigades and NKVD units, he came to a halt.

Second Panzer Army side-stepped Tula to the east; somehow they staggered on to Venev by the 24th, and actually reached Kashira. There 17th Panzer Division handled Boldin's 50th Army roughly, drawing Zhukov's attention, and one of his last reserves, the 2nd Cavalry Corps. This formation, which was renamed 1st Guards Cavalry Corps on the 26th, received substantial close air support, and arrived in Kashira just

Most German wheeled vehicles did not perform well in harsh weather conditions, as shown in this photograph of German troops struggling to push a Krupp L2H143 1.5-ton light truck along a frozen Russian road. (Nik Cornish at Stavka)

hours before 17th Panzer Division. Belov's cavalrymen overran that division's scattered outposts – and then disappeared into Army Group Center's rear areas, for a five-month rampage.

At Tula, Boldin's men held on grimly, and on November 27–28 Guderian sent what remained of 3rd and 4th Panzer Divisions on a counterclockwise sweep north of the city. Their armor was consolidated into Kampfgruppe Eberbach, which numbered 110 tanks on the 17th but only 32 a week later. He likewise ordered XLIII Army Corps to come clockwise from the south in an attempt to encircle this obstacle. Personally leading the advance, the star Panzer general experienced at first hand the difficulties faced by his men fighting in temperatures as low as -35˚C. The 340th Rifle and 112th Tank Divisions held open Tula's last corridor to the outside despite Guderian's efforts. On November 27, Guderian added his voice to the growing chorus of Army Group Center generals frustrated at Von Kluge's inactivity. Guderian said that he could not continue assaulting "if the right wing of Fourth Army for its part does not assume the offensive without delay"; but Von Bock told Guderian's chief of staff that such an attack was "out of the question."

Meanwhile, on the army group's extreme right, the Second Army (with ColGen Rudolf Schmidt replaced the ailing Von Weichs) shoved aside the Soviet 3rd and 13th Armies and made for Voronezh. However, the usual combination of terrible weather, weak logistics and Red Army resistance, plus poor co-ordination with the neighboring Sixth Army (Army Group South's left flank) conspired to bring Schmidt's men to a halt by the end of the month, well short of his objective.

Von Bock versus Zhukov: Center

Supposedly the *Schwerpunkt*, the Fourth Army fought a defensive battle while the armor attacked on its flanks. Zhukov felt secure about this critical sector; he would concentrate on the wings while keeping a wary eye on the expected attack up the middle.

While Third and Fourth Panzer Groups advanced early in the offensive, Von Kluge attacked with his left on November 18–19.

Black smoke billows from a Ju 88 medium bomber at the Orel airfield, shortly after a low-level attack by the Soviet Air Force. (Courtesy of the Central Museum of the Armed Forces Moscow)

The closer the Germans got to Moscow, the farther they were from their supply sources, and the closer the Soviets were to theirs. Here two M1937 45mm antitank guns are manned by their well-equipped crews. (Elukka)

However, according to Von Bock, the right wing of Fourth Army was "very serious and precarious." Von Kluge paraded a series of excuses for his inaction, to the extreme annoyance of Halder and Von Bock. For over a year the German Army had been anticipating the final assault against Stalin's capital, and now that the moment had arrived the commander of the main effort would not move.

Von Kluge finally stirred himself, and attacked on December 1 in the direction of Naro–Fominsk, with XX Army Corps flanked by LVII Panzer (total tank strength: 70) and IX Army Corps. Initial success against the 43rd Army offered a slight glimmer of hope when it looked as if 258th Infantry Division might achieve a breakthrough, hitting the second-echelon 5th Army defending the Minsk–Moscow highway; but Zhukov anticipated the blow and had a counter. On the assault's second day 33rd Army (LtGen M.G. Yefremov) counterattacked with the 5th and 11th Tank Brigades plus one tank and two ski battalions.

T-34s and Sturmgeschütze hunted each other through the villages, which Soviet aircraft bombed simply to deprive the invaders of any shelter. The Germans were soon driven back, in some disorder, to their start lines. Von Bock did not know what to think; on December 2 he told Von Kluge, Hoepner and Reinhardt that the Soviets were ready to break, but a day later he told Halder that he "doubted the success" of the Moscow operation.

Immediately following the battles for Viazma and Bryansk, Von Bock had had the defenders of Moscow reeling. When he did eventually resume offensive operations in mid-November, he could only do so in fits and starts. Having already given the Soviets weeks to catch their balance, he now attacked sequentially over a period of weeks – which allowed Zhukov to parry in a corresponding fashion.

During the *Ostheer's* last lunge toward Moscow, Third and Fourth Panzer groups advanced between 50 and 60 miles, finally arriving 12–20 miles from the Kremlin. Their pressure near Yakhroma made November 27 a real day of crisis for Zhukov, although neither side was fully aware of the fact at the time. The relatively under-resourced Second Panzer Army never got as close to Moscow, and after Tula took no objective of even operational value. Guderian, Hoepner and Reinhardt all clamored to be designated as the assault's *Schwerpunkt* (the Wehrmacht could only resource one at a time), while the man given that distinction did not know what to do with it. They all complained about Von Kluge, who in turn complained about them; Von Bock could not manage his unruly subordinates.

Only at the Orsha conference Halder had realized the desperate condition of the Wehrmacht in Russia. In a juxtaposition of points of view, the Chief of Staff then decided that the Germans must only threaten Moscow, not capture it; Hitler overrode Halder, stating that they needed it. This bizarre relationship between Germany's senior political and military leaders hamstrung Operation *Typhoon*. By contrast, at the beginning of *Typhoon* the Red Army defense of Moscow suffered from apparently terminal disorganization; six weeks later Zhukov had undisputed command of the entire theater and Stalin's full confidence. Only when it was far too late – by November 29, to judge from Von Bock's diary – did the Germans acknowledge the Soviets' "huge reserves."

Stalin, Stavka and the entire Soviet command structure had been waiting for *Typhoon* (and by extension, *Barbarossa*) to reach its culminating point so that they could begin their general winter counteroffensive. Between November 29 and 30, Zhukov briefed the dictator on the attack that would mark the end of both German advances and Moscow's danger. The anemic Army Group Center, with its long, indefensible lines of supply and uncovered flanks, was ripe for the taking.

CONCLUSIONS

ARMY GROUP CENTER

Von Bock's army group began the invasion with almost every advantage, while Pavlov's West Front could hardly have been in a worse position. In a matter of days Von Bock's men had trapped a third of a million Red Army soldiers at Minsk. Two weeks later they were on the verge of closing another, larger and more strategically significant *Kessel* at Smolensk. Everywhere, Soviet countermeasures failed, and a drive on Moscow looked unstoppable. However, Moscow did not rate high on the list of objectives for *Barbarossa*: in the pertinent documents the capital is mentioned almost as an afterthought.

All did not go perfectly for Army Group Center, but initial successes concealed *Barbarossa*'s flaws from both combatants and the wider world. Logistics were a limiting factor from its earliest days. Various pockets took longer and required more mechanized forces to reduce than planners expected. Leaders like Guderian pursued individual goals. Third Panzer Group was expected to accomplish too much relative to its resources: to continue the advance eastward, reduce encirclements, and close the northern flank with Von Leeb.

Many German generals did think in terms of taking Moscow, chief among them Franz Halder, but even he was far from consistent. Many commentators have taken the Germans to task for not capturing the city. While taking the enemy's capital is intuitively attractive, there is no proof that occupying Moscow would have led directly to the collapse of the USSR, notwithstanding clichés about the "seat of centralized Soviet power" or the "hub of the Soviet transportation net." As Timoshenko told the Supreme Defense Council: "If Germany succeeds in taking Moscow that is obviously a grave disappointment for us, but it by no means disrupts our grand strategy; that alone will not win [them] the war."

In fact, it seems that the closer the Germans got to Moscow the more *Barbarossa* lost its compass. After Smolensk they surrendered the strategic initiative in the center to regain it on the flanks. The turn south of Guderian's Panzer group reaped a huge harvest in the form of history's greatest encirclement at Kiev; the half measure of sending only part of Hoth's Third Panzer north did not have nearly the same impact.

Meanwhile, first Timoshenko and later Zhukov gladly picked up the initiative dropped by the Germans. Their counterattacks achieved no more than the temporary liberation of Yelnia – which turned out not to be essential to the assault on Moscow, and therefore did not justify German efforts to hold it.

The speed and ferocity of Operation *Typhoon* surprised the Soviets once again; however, first exhaustion and logistic weakness, and then the effects of seasonal weather terminally slowed the advance. The Soviet defense

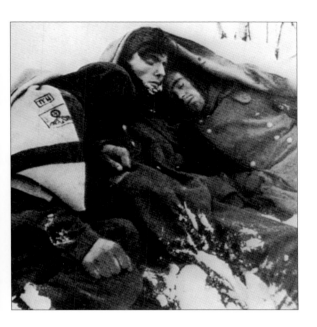

**Not even a coffin lid for shelter...
Doubtless trying to share body
warmth, these German soldiers
froze to death in their sleep
beside a road. (Podzun)**

crumbled as before, but it did not collapse into a confused rout. As throughout *Barbarossa*, the Red Army took advantage of every German pause and weakness. For more than two years, up to and including the battles of Viazma–Bryansk, the Germans had prevailed everywhere they chose to create a *Schwerpunkt*. But in November and December 1941, for the first time in such an enterprise, they failed.

Operation *Barbarossa* as a whole

Barbarossa's weaknesses were principally the failure to set clear objectives for operations beyond the Dvina–Dnepr line; lack of consensus among the national leadership; sanguine planning, weakened by poor intelligence; and simply the realities of a medium-size country invading the world's largest nation. When these factors are balanced against the ruthless Soviet leadership, a tenacious Red Army defense, terrible weather and terrain, and a new and talented generation of generals led by Zhukov, one can see that the Germans had to perform flawlessly if they were to win in Russia.

At the start of *Barbarossa*, Hitler told an aide: "At the beginning of each campaign one pushes a door into a dark, unseen room. One can never know what is hiding inside." Yet the relative ease of their campaigns prior to *Barbarossa* led to a false sense of German invincibility among many (although not all) Wehrmacht leaders and outside observers. Planning by both combatants was strikingly similar in that each appeared to be divorced from reality. After the war one German general wrote that the campaign's planning "rested upon the assumption that German military power was, and would continue to be, irresistible."[5] Many of *Barbarossa*'s senior leaders had served on the Russian Front during 1914–17, and knew that the Tsar's bungling army had still fought that of the Kaiser to a stalemate. Yet these same men believed a force smaller than that required to subdue France in 1940 would only need a couple of months to conquer the earth's largest nation and army. Meanwhile, Soviet leaders naively expected to be counterattacking deep into the German rear within days or weeks of an invasion.

By the spring of 1941 each military had evidently developed some respect for the other; Germany essentially doubled the number of divisions it considered necessary, while the USSR mobilized an additional half-million men the month before *Barbarossa*. Not wanting to damage German civilian morale as had happened a generation earlier, Hitler maintained domestic goods manufacture over ordnance production until well past 1941. Although the Luftwaffe in the East was spread very thin, Hitler kept two bomber *Geschwader* facing Great Britain despite their lacking a clear mission. For his part, Stalin discounted unmistakable signs of the German build-up as just another skirmish in the war of nerves that had dominated Europe for five years.

Following long tradition, the *Ostheer* concentrated on destroying enemy formations rather than seizing terrain objectives. This doctrine made it very difficult to judge success, especially in view of the Wehrmacht's pitiable strategic intelligence capabilities. The Wehrmacht also concentrated on operations to the detriment of logistics, but *Barbarossa* devoured materiel at a rate unanticipated by all but the direst estimates.

Judging by his diary entries, German successes surprised even Halder. The Wehrmacht assaulted in strength everywhere along the massive front, to the extent that the Red Army could not discern its main effort, thus naturally complicating the defense.

In the first half of July, Panzer groups were within striking distance of Leningrad, Smolensk and Kiev. Soviet counterattacks following prewar plans all failed because of a pattern of poor command and control, inexperience, and German operational and tactical acumen. The Red Army then initiated a second wave of countermoves, most notably those bearing Timoshenko's name, along the Moscow axis. Although many forces earmarked for operational purposes were squandered on tactical missions, these attacks signaled that the Soviets would not give up the Dvina–Dnepr line without a fight.

By the first week of August the Uman and Smolensk pockets marked victories by Army Groups South and Center. In the north, however, operational triumph eluded the Germans. Following the capture of Novgorod, Von Manstein suggested reinforcing success by sending his armored corps north behind that of Reinhardt. Hoepner seconded the recommendation, but Von Leeb ignored it, and instead ordered the costly and time-consuming assault across the upper Luga river. Although Army Group North eventually cut off the USSR's second city from overland communication, Von Leeb's attack essentially halted at this point.

By the end of July the campaign had stalled, as the Führer argued with his generals over the prosecution of its second phase. While he issued a series of often contradictory Führer Directives, commanders on the ground fought *Barbarossa* as they saw fit. The generals renewed calls to assault Moscow, while the dictator wanted action on the flanks. The campaign moved forward, albeit rudderless, until Hitler resolved the matter in late August.

Never in favor of a direct attack on Moscow, Hitler had strategic reasons for taking decisive action on *Barbarossa*'s wings. Success at either extreme could possibly bring Turkey into the war or motivate Finland to redouble its efforts. Germany needed every last resource of the Ukraine. Equally, the *Ostheer* could not ignore the mass of troops, among the Red Army's best, sitting on the boundary between Army Groups Center and South. Once the decision to go to Kiev had been made, Guderian moved south quickly. Stalin, focused on Moscow and, distracted by Luftwaffe bombing of the capital, missed the move. Von Kleist's Panzer group, held up on the Irpen river (and thus giving the Soviets greater opportunity to evacuate Ukrainian industry), sought the line of least resistance on his right, and thereby created a huge salient. These two armored jaws slamming shut at Lochvitsa represented the zenith of German operational art, but victory at Kiev was soon offset by superior Soviet force generation.

While Army Group Center had been fairly static on either side of Yelnia, the Soviets took the offensive and proved that they were not beaten. During the second half of September the German generals demonstrated how fast they could move when they wanted to, by reorienting two and a half Panzer groups plus numerous infantry formations from the Leningrad and Kiev areas to the Moscow axis. Von Bock's last great victory came at Viazma–Bryansk. He was then abruptly slowed, by weather (first in the

The battlefield today; the author seated before an SU-152 assault gun at the Chernigov war memorial in July 2005. Casual historian beware; the map in the background shows the 1943 liberation of the city, but no mention is made of its loss on September 7 1941. (Author's collection)

form of mud and later by sub-zero cold) combined with the "four horsemen" of Nazi strategic overstretch: troop exhaustion, personnel and materiel attrition, anemic logistics, and the continuing inability to settle on attainable objectives.

Toward the end of November, Von Bock's men stumbled toward Moscow in the well-known *Flucht nach vorn*. Von Leeb at Tikhvin and Volkhov, and Von Rundstedt at Rostov, did the same. Whether or not the capture of Moscow would truly have represented a checkmate, it never occurred. Encircling the city represented an orthodox but equally impossible solution (as subsequent events at Leningrad and Stalingrad would indicate). Even though history's greatest encirclement at Kiev did not win the war for Germany, it has been argued that taking Moscow would have; but there is much evidence to the contrary – that the Soviets would simply have kept on fighting east of their capital.

Even with the advantages of hindsight, at no point before about mid-November 1941 is *Barbarossa*'s conclusion clear. If one concentrates on operations and ignores German logistics and the disparity in force generation, it may seem that until the end of that month the *Ostheer* might have had a chance of winning. In the end, however, the two sides were just too unevenly matched.

In June the balance sheet seemed to favor the invaders, as clearly as it appeared to favor the defenders in December. Did the Germans cling too long to the anachronistic concept of the Napoleonic "decisive battle"? None of their spectacular list of victories at Minsk, Ivanskoye, Uman, Smolensk, Kiev, Viazma–Bryansk, Melitopol, the Crimea and elsewhere delivered the hoped-for knockout blow against the Red Army. German victory required success in destroying the Red Army and capturing Leningrad, Moscow and the Ukraine – not just one or two of these objectives. That was clearly beyond their capabilities. The constant, random Soviet counterattacks, the death-by-a-thousand-cuts technique, eventually saved the USSR. As *Barbarossa* went on, wherever Zhukov showed up, German fortunes faded. When the Nazi–Soviet War transitioned from one of maneuver to one of attrition, victory moved decisively beyond Hitler's grasp.

BIBLIOGRAPHY

Andrew, Christopher, *The Sword and the Shield,* Basic Books, 1999
Bartov, Omer, *Germany's War and the Holocaust,* Cornell U., 2003
Baumann, Hans, *Die 35 Infanteriedivision,* G. Braun, 1964
Bergstrom, C. & A. Mikhailov, *Black Cross, Red Star,* Pacifica Military, 2000
Beyersdorff, Ernst, *Geschichte der 110 Infanteriedivision,* Podzun, 1965
Blankenhagen, Wilhelm, *Im Zeichen des Schwertes,* Giebel, 1982
Bock, Fedor von, *The War Diary,* Schiffer, 1996
Boog, Horst, et al., *Germany in the Second World War, Vol.IV: Attack on the Soviet Union,*
    Clarendon Press, 1998
Chickering & Forster, eds., *Shadows of Total War,* German History Institute, 2003
Chales de Beaulieu, Walter, *Generaloberst Erich Hoepner,* Vowinckel, 1969
Childers & Caplan, eds., *Reevaluating the Third Reich,* Holmes & Meyer, 1993
Dunn, Walter, *Hitler's Nemesis,* Praeger, 1994
Erickson, John, *The Road to Stalingrad,* Yale U., 1999
Glantz, David, *Barbarossa,* Tempus, 2001
Glantz, David, *Before Stalingrad,* Tempus, 2003
Glantz, David, *The Initial Period of the War,* Frank Cass, 2004
Glantz, David, numerous self-published booklets and atlases
Guderian, Heinz, *Panzer Leader,* Ballantine, 1957
Haupt, Werner, *Army Group Center,* Schiffer, 1997
Haupt, Werner, *Die 260 Infanteriedivision,* Podzun, 1970
Haupt, Werner, *Die Deutschen vor Moskau,* Podzun, 1996
Haywood, Joel, *Stopped at Stalingrad,* U. of Kansas, 1998
Hertlein, Wilhelm, *Chronik der 7 Infanteriedivision,* Bruckmann, 1984
Hossbach, Friedrich, *Infanterie im Ostfeldzug,* Giebel, 1951
Hoth, Hermann, *Panzer Operationen,* Vowinkel, 1956
Kershaw, Ian, *Hitler: Nemesis,* Norton, 2000
Knoblesdorff, Otto von, *Geschichte der niedersachsischen 19 Panzerdivision,* Podzun, 1958
Kokoshin, Andrei, *Soviet Strategic Thought 1917–91,* MIT Press, 1998
Komar, Gary, *Operation Barbarossa – The Case Against Moscow,* unpublished MS
Kozhevnikov, M.N., *Command and Staff of the Red Army Air Force,* USAF, 1977
Laffin, John, *Jackboot,* Cassell, 1966
Luttichau, Charles von, unpublished MS
Megargee, Geoffrey, *Inside Hitler's High Command,* U. of Kansas, 2002
Merker, Ludwig, *Das Buch der 78 Sturmdivision,* Kameradshilfswerk, n/d
Meyer-Detring, Wilhelm, *Die 137 Infanteriedivision,* Kameradschaft, 1962
Murphy, David, *What Stalin Knew,* Yale U., 2005
Neumann, Joachim, *Die 4 Panzerdivision,* Bernard und Graefe, 1957
Newton, Steven, *German Battle Tactics on the Russian Front,* Schiffer, 1997
Oehmichen, Hermann, *Der Weg der 87 Infanteriedivision,* Selbstverlag, 1969
Overy, Richard, *Russia's War,* TV Books, 1997
Paul, Wolfgang, *Brennpunkte,* Biblio Verlag, 1984
Paul, Wolfgang, *Geschichte der 18 Panzerdivision,* Preussische Militär Verlag, 1989
Plato, Anton von, *Die Geschichte der 5 Panzerdivision,* Walhalla, 1978
Pleshakov, Constantine, *Stalin's Folly,* Houghton Mifflin, 2005
Plocher, Hermann, *The German Air Force versus Russia,* Arno Press, 1967
Pons, Shivo, *Stalin and the Inevitable War,* Frank Cass, 2002
Reinhardt, Klaus, *Moscow, The Turning Point,* Berg, 1992
Scheibert, Horst, *Die Gespenster Division,* Pallas, 1981
Schmidt, August, *Geschichte der 10 Division,* Podzun, 1963
Seaton, Albert, *Stalin's War,* Combined, 1998
Stephan, Robert, *Stalin's Secret War,* U. of Kansas, 2004
Taylor, Brian, *Barbarossa to Berlin, Vol. 1,* Spellmount, 2003
Warlimont, Walter, *Inside Hitler's Headquarters,* Presidio, 1991
Weinberg, Gerhard, ed., *Hitler's Second Book,* Enigma, 2003
Willmott, H.P., *The Great Crusade,* Free Press, 1988
Ziemke, Earl, *Moscow to Stalingrad,* Military Heritage Press, 1988

INDEX